C-2967 CAREER EXAMINATION SERIES

THIS IS YOUR **PASSBOOK**® FOR ...

ACCOUNTANT II

212 Michael Drive, Syosset, NY 11791
(516) 921-8888 • www.passbooks.com
E-mail: info@passbooks.com

PUBLISHED IN THE UNITED STATES OF AMERICA

PASSBOOK® SERIES

THE *PASSBOOK® SERIES* has been created to prepare applicants and candidates for the ultimate academic battlefield – the examination room.

At some time in our lives, each and every one of us may be required to take an examination – for validation, matriculation, admission, qualification, registration, certification, or licensure.

Based on the assumption that every applicant or candidate has met the basic formal educational standards, has taken the required number of courses, and read the necessary texts, the *PASSBOOK® SERIES* furnishes the one special preparation which may assure passing with confidence, instead of failing with insecurity. Examination questions – together with answers – are furnished as the basic vehicle for study so that the mysteries of the examination and its compounding difficulties may be eliminated or diminished by a sure method.

This book is meant to help you pass your examination provided that you qualify and are serious in your objective.

The entire field is reviewed through the huge store of content information which is succinctly presented through a provocative and challenging approach – the question-and-answer method.

A climate of success is established by furnishing the correct answers at the end of each test.

You soon learn to recognize types of questions, forms of questions, and patterns of questioning. You may even begin to anticipate expected outcomes.

You perceive that many questions are repeated or adapted so that you can gain acute insights, which may enable you to score many sure points.

You learn how to confront new questions, or types of questions, and to attack them confidently and work out the correct answers.

You note objectives and emphases, and recognize pitfalls and dangers, so that you may make positive educational adjustments.

Moreover, you are kept fully informed in relation to new concepts, methods, practices, and directions in the field.

You discover that you arre actually taking the examination all the time: you are preparing for the examination by "taking" an examination, not by reading extraneous and/or supererogatory textbooks.

In short, this PASSBOOK®, used directedly, should be an important factor in helping you to pass your test.

ACCOUNTANT II

DUTIES:

Performs complex and difficult professional accounting work. Supervises the maintenance of expenditures and budgetary control accounts and prepares reports relating to account status; performs related duties as required.

SUBJECT OF EXAMINATION:

The written test is designed to evaluate knowledge, skills and /or abilities in the following areas:

1. **General accounting** - These questions test for knowledge of the general accounting principles and practices used in the preparation of financial statements, in the recording and reporting of financial transactions, and in financial decision-making. Candidates will be required to demonstrate a current knowledge of Generally Accepted Accounting Principles (GAAP). Knowledge of computerized information systems as it applies to accounting may be required.
2. **General auditing** - These questions test for knowledge of the principles and procedures involved in substantiating and examining transactions and financial statements. It will require knowledge of auditing techniques and Generally Accepted Auditing Standards (GAAS). Knowledge of the use of computerized accounting or auditing systems as it pertains to auditing may be required. Questions relating to internal controls applicable to manual and computerized accounting systems may be included.
3. **Governmental accounting** - These questions test for knowledge of the accounting practices employed to provide financial information used in determining and forecasting the condition of governmental units, and used for monitoring governmental performance, in terms of legal, contractual and fiduciary requirements. These questions will test for knowledge of and familiarity with common governmental funds, appropriation and encumbrance accounting, accounting for revenue and expenditures, and other aspects of accounting relating to the governmental sector.
4. **Preparing written material** - These questions test for the ability to present information clearly and accurately, and to organize paragraphs logically and comprehensibly. For some questions, you will be given information in two or three sentences followed by four restatements of the information. You must then choose the best version. For other questions, you will be given paragraphs with their sentences out of order. You must then choose, from four suggestions, the best order for the sentences.
5. **Supervision** - These questions test for knowledge of the principles and practices employed in planning, organizing, and controlling the activities of a work unit toward predetermined objectives. The concepts covered, usually in a situational question format, include such topics as assigning and reviewing work; evaluating performance; maintaining work standards; motivating and developing subordinates; implementing procedural change; increasing efficiency; and dealing with problems of absenteeism, morale, and discipline.
6. **Understanding and interpreting tabular material** - These questions test your ability to understand, analyze, and use the internal logic of data presented in tabular form. You may be asked to perform tasks such as completing tables, drawing conclusions from them, analyzing data trends or interrelationships, and revising or combining data sets. The concepts of rate, ratio, and proportion are tested. Mathematical operations are simple, and computational speed is not a major factor in the test.

HOW TO TAKE A TEST

I. YOU MUST PASS AN EXAMINATION

A. WHAT EVERY CANDIDATE SHOULD KNOW

Examination applicants often ask us for help in preparing for the written test. What can I study in advance? What kinds of questions will be asked? How will the test be given? How will the papers be graded?

As an applicant for a civil service examination, you may be wondering about some of these things. Our purpose here is to suggest effective methods of advance study and to describe civil service examinations.

Your chances for success on this examination can be increased if you know how to prepare. Those "pre-examination jitters" can be reduced if you know what to expect. You can even experience an adventure in good citizenship if you know why civil service exams are given.

B. WHY ARE CIVIL SERVICE EXAMINATIONS GIVEN?

Civil service examinations are important to you in two ways. As a citizen, you want public jobs filled by employees who know how to do their work. As a job seeker, you want a fair chance to compete for that job on an equal footing with other candidates. The best-known means of accomplishing this two-fold goal is the competitive examination.

Exams are widely publicized throughout the nation. They may be administered for jobs in federal, state, city, municipal, town or village governments or agencies.

Any citizen may apply, with some limitations, such as the age or residence of applicants. Your experience and education may be reviewed to see whether you meet the requirements for the particular examination. When these requirements exist, they are reasonable and applied consistently to all applicants. Thus, a competitive examination may cause you some uneasiness now, but it is your privilege and safeguard.

C. HOW ARE CIVIL SERVICE EXAMS DEVELOPED?

Examinations are carefully written by trained technicians who are specialists in the field known as "psychological measurement," in consultation with recognized authorities in the field of work that the test will cover. These experts recommend the subject matter areas or skills to be tested; only those knowledges or skills important to your success on the job are included. The most reliable books and source materials available are used as references. Together, the experts and technicians judge the difficulty level of the questions.

Test technicians know how to phrase questions so that the problem is clearly stated. Their ethics do not permit "trick" or "catch" questions. Questions may have been tried out on sample groups, or subjected to statistical analysis, to determine their usefulness.

Written tests are often used in combination with performance tests, ratings of training and experience, and oral interviews. All of these measures combine to form the best-known means of finding the right person for the right job.

II. HOW TO PASS THE WRITTEN TEST

A. NATURE OF THE EXAMINATION

To prepare intelligently for civil service examinations, you should know how they differ from school examinations you have taken. In school you were assigned certain definite pages to read or subjects to cover. The examination questions were quite detailed and usually emphasized memory. Civil service exams, on the other hand, try to discover your present ability to perform the duties of a position, plus your potentiality to learn these duties. In other words, a civil service exam attempts to predict how successful you will be. Questions cover such a broad area that they cannot be as minute and detailed as school exam questions.

In the public service similar kinds of work, or positions, are grouped together in one "class." This process is known as *position-classification*. All the positions in a class are paid according to the salary range for that class. One class title covers all of these positions, and they are all tested by the same examination.

B. FOUR BASIC STEPS

1) Study the announcement

How, then, can you know what subjects to study? Our best answer is: "Learn as much as possible about the class of positions for which you've applied." The exam will test the knowledge, skills and abilities needed to do the work.

Your most valuable source of information about the position you want is the official exam announcement. This announcement lists the training and experience qualifications. Check these standards and apply only if you come reasonably close to meeting them.

The brief description of the position in the examination announcement offers some clues to the subjects which will be tested. Think about the job itself. Review the duties in your mind. Can you perform them, or are there some in which you are rusty? Fill in the blank spots in your preparation.

Many jurisdictions preview the written test in the exam announcement by including a section called "Knowledge and Abilities Required," "Scope of the Examination," or some similar heading. Here you will find out specifically what fields will be tested.

2) Review your own background

Once you learn in general what the position is all about, and what you need to know to do the work, ask yourself which subjects you already know fairly well and which need improvement. You may wonder whether to concentrate on improving your strong areas or on building some background in your fields of weakness. When the announcement has specified "some knowledge" or "considerable knowledge," or has used adjectives like "beginning principles of..." or "advanced ... methods," you can get a clue as to the number and difficulty of questions to be asked in any given field. More questions, and hence broader coverage, would be included for those subjects which are more important in the work. Now weigh your strengths and weaknesses against the job requirements and prepare accordingly.

3) Determine the level of the position

Another way to tell how intensively you should prepare is to understand the level of the job for which you are applying. Is it the entering level? In other words, is this the position in which beginners in a field of work are hired? Or is it an intermediate or advanced level? Sometimes this is indicated by such words as "Junior" or "Senior" in the class title. Other jurisdictions use Roman numerals to designate the level – Clerk I, Clerk II, for example. The word "Supervisor" sometimes appears in the title. If the level is not indicated by the title, check the description of duties. Will you be working under very close supervision, or will you have responsibility for independent decisions in this work?

4) Choose appropriate study materials

Now that you know the subjects to be examined and the relative amount of each subject to be covered, you can choose suitable study materials. For beginning level jobs, or even advanced ones, if you have a pronounced weakness in some aspect of your training, read a modern, standard textbook in that field. Be sure it is up to date and has general coverage. Such books are normally available at your library, and the librarian will be glad to help you locate one. For entry-level positions, questions of appropriate difficulty are chosen – neither highly advanced questions, nor those too simple. Such questions require careful thought but not advanced training.

If the position for which you are applying is technical or advanced, you will read more advanced, specialized material. If you are already familiar with the basic principles of your field, elementary textbooks would waste your time. Concentrate on advanced textbooks and technical periodicals. Think through the concepts and review difficult problems in your field.

These are all general sources. You can get more ideas on your own initiative, following these leads. For example, training manuals and publications of the government agency which employs workers in your field can be useful, particularly for technical and professional positions. A letter or visit to the government department involved may result in more specific study suggestions, and certainly will provide you with a more definite idea of the exact nature of the position you are seeking.

III. KINDS OF TESTS

Tests are used for purposes other than measuring knowledge and ability to perform specified duties. For some positions, it is equally important to test ability to make adjustments to new situations or to profit from training. In others, basic mental abilities not dependent on information are essential. Questions which test these things may not appear as pertinent to the duties of the position as those which test for knowledge and information. Yet they are often highly important parts of a fair examination. For very general questions, it is almost impossible to help you direct your study efforts. What we can do is to point out some of the more common of these general abilities needed in public service positions and describe some typical questions.

1) General information

Broad, general information has been found useful for predicting job success in some kinds of work. This is tested in a variety of ways, from vocabulary lists to questions about current events. Basic background in some field of work, such as sociology or economics, may be sampled in a group of questions. Often these are principles which have become familiar to most persons through exposure rather than through formal training. It is difficult to advise you how to study for these questions; being alert to the world around you is our best suggestion.

2) Verbal ability

An example of an ability needed in many positions is verbal or language ability. Verbal ability is, in brief, the ability to use and understand words. Vocabulary and grammar tests are typical measures of this ability. Reading comprehension or paragraph interpretation questions are common in many kinds of civil service tests. You are given a paragraph of written material and asked to find its central meaning.

3) Numerical ability

Number skills can be tested by the familiar arithmetic problem, by checking paired lists of numbers to see which are alike and which are different, or by interpreting charts and graphs. In the latter test, a graph may be printed in the test booklet which you are asked to use as the basis for answering questions.

4) Observation

A popular test for law-enforcement positions is the observation test. A picture is shown to you for several minutes, then taken away. Questions about the picture test your ability to observe both details and larger elements.

5) Following directions

In many positions in the public service, the employee must be able to carry out written instructions dependably and accurately. You may be given a chart with several columns, each column listing a variety of information. The questions require you to carry out directions involving the information given in the chart.

6) Skills and aptitudes

Performance tests effectively measure some manual skills and aptitudes. When the skill is one in which you are trained, such as typing or shorthand, you can practice. These tests are often very much like those given in business school or high school courses. For many of the other skills and aptitudes, however, no short-time preparation can be made. Skills and abilities natural to you or that you have developed throughout your lifetime are being tested.

Many of the general questions just described provide all the data needed to answer the questions and ask you to use your reasoning ability to find the answers. Your best preparation for these tests, as well as for tests of facts and ideas, is to be at your physical and mental best. You, no doubt, have your own methods of getting into an exam-taking mood and keeping “in shape.” The next section lists some ideas on this subject.

IV. KINDS OF QUESTIONS

Only rarely is the “essay” question, which you answer in narrative form, used in civil service tests. Civil service tests are usually of the short-answer type. Full instructions for answering these questions will be given to you at the examination. But in case this is your first experience with short-answer questions and separate answer sheets, here is what you need to know:

1) Multiple-choice Questions

Most popular of the short-answer questions is the "multiple choice" or "best answer" question. It can be used, for example, to test for factual knowledge, ability to solve problems or judgment in meeting situations found at work.

A multiple-choice question is normally one of three types—

- It can begin with an incomplete statement followed by several possible endings. You are to find the one ending which *best* completes the statement, although some of the others may not be entirely wrong.
- It can also be a complete statement in the form of a question which is answered by choosing one of the statements listed.
- It can be in the form of a problem – again you select the best answer.

Here is an example of a multiple-choice question with a discussion which should give you some clues as to the method for choosing the right answer:

When an employee has a complaint about his assignment, the action which will *best* help him overcome his difficulty is to

A. discuss his difficulty with his coworkers
B. take the problem to the head of the organization
C. take the problem to the person who gave him the assignment
D. say nothing to anyone about his complaint

In answering this question, you should study each of the choices to find which is best. Consider choice "A" – Certainly an employee may discuss his complaint with fellow employees, but no change or improvement can result, and the complaint remains unresolved. Choice "B" is a poor choice since the head of the organization probably does not know what assignment you have been given, and taking your problem to him is known as "going over the head" of the supervisor. The supervisor, or person who made the assignment, is the person who can clarify it or correct any injustice. Choice "C" is, therefore, correct. To say nothing, as in choice "D," is unwise. Supervisors have and interest in knowing the problems employees are facing, and the employee is seeking a solution to his problem.

2) True/False Questions

The "true/false" or "right/wrong" form of question is sometimes used. Here a complete statement is given. Your job is to decide whether the statement is right or wrong.

SAMPLE: A roaming cell-phone call to a nearby city costs less than a non-roaming call to a distant city.

This statement is wrong, or false, since roaming calls are more expensive.

This is not a complete list of all possible question forms, although most of the others are variations of these common types. You will always get complete directions for answering questions. Be sure you understand *how* to mark your answers – ask questions until you do.

V. RECORDING YOUR ANSWERS

Computer terminals are used more and more today for many different kinds of exams.

For an examination with very few applicants, you may be told to record your answers in the test booklet itself. Separate answer sheets are much more common. If this separate answer sheet is to be scored by machine – and this is often the case – it is highly important that you mark your answers correctly in order to get credit.

An electronic scoring machine is often used in civil service offices because of the speed with which papers can be scored. Machine-scored answer sheets must be marked with a pencil, which will be given to you. This pencil has a high graphite content which responds to the electronic scoring machine. As a matter of fact, stray dots may register as answers, so do not let your pencil rest on the answer sheet while you are pondering the correct answer. Also, if your pencil lead breaks or is otherwise defective, ask for another.

Since the answer sheet will be dropped in a slot in the scoring machine, be careful not to bend the corners or get the paper crumpled.

The answer sheet normally has five vertical columns of numbers, with 30 numbers to a column. These numbers correspond to the question numbers in your test booklet. After each number, going across the page are four or five pairs of dotted lines. These short dotted lines have small letters or numbers above them. The first two pairs may also have a "T" or "F" above the letters. This indicates that the first two pairs only are to be used if the questions are of the true-false type. If the questions are multiple choice, disregard the "T" and "F" and pay attention only to the small letters or numbers.

Answer your questions in the manner of the sample that follows:

32. The largest city in the United States is
    - A. Washington, D.C.
    - B. New York City
    - C. Chicago
    - D. Detroit
    - E. San Francisco

1) Choose the answer you think is best. (New York City is the largest, so "B" is correct.)
2) Find the row of dotted lines numbered the same as the question you are answering. (Find row number 32)
3) Find the pair of dotted lines corresponding to the answer. (Find the pair of lines under the mark "B.")
4) Make a solid black mark between the dotted lines.

VI. BEFORE THE TEST

Common sense will help you find procedures to follow to get ready for an examination. Too many of us, however, overlook these sensible measures. Indeed, nervousness and fatigue have been found to be the most serious reasons why applicants fail to do their best on civil service tests. Here is a list of reminders:

- Begin your preparation early – Don't wait until the last minute to go scurrying around for books and materials or to find out what the position is all about.
- Prepare continuously – An hour a night for a week is better than an all-night cram session. This has been definitely established. What is more, a night a week for a month will return better dividends than crowding your study into a shorter period of time.
- Locate the place of the exam – You have been sent a notice telling you when and where to report for the examination. If the location is in a different town or otherwise unfamiliar to you, it would be well to inquire the best route and learn something about the building.
- Relax the night before the test – Allow your mind to rest. Do not study at all that night. Plan some mild recreation or diversion; then go to bed early and get a good night's sleep.
- Get up early enough to make a leisurely trip to the place for the test – This way unforeseen events, traffic snarls, unfamiliar buildings, etc. will not upset you.
- Dress comfortably – A written test is not a fashion show. You will be known by number and not by name, so wear something comfortable.
- Leave excess paraphernalia at home – Shopping bags and odd bundles will get in your way. You need bring only the items mentioned in the official notice you received; usually everything you need is provided. Do not bring reference books to the exam. They will only confuse those last minutes and be taken away from you when in the test room.
- Arrive somewhat ahead of time – If because of transportation schedules you must get there very early, bring a newspaper or magazine to take your mind off yourself while waiting.
- Locate the examination room – When you have found the proper room, you will be directed to the seat or part of the room where you will sit. Sometimes you are given a sheet of instructions to read while you are waiting. Do not fill out any forms until you are told to do so; just read them and be prepared.
- Relax and prepare to listen to the instructions
- If you have any physical problem that may keep you from doing your best, be sure to tell the test administrator. If you are sick or in poor health, you really cannot do your best on the exam. You can come back and take the test some other time.

VII. AT THE TEST

The day of the test is here and you have the test booklet in your hand. The temptation to get going is very strong. Caution! There is more to success than knowing the right answers. You must know how to identify your papers and understand variations in the type of short-answer question used in this particular examination. Follow these suggestions for maximum results from your efforts:

1) Cooperate with the monitor

The test administrator has a duty to create a situation in which you can be as much at ease as possible. He will give instructions, tell you when to begin, check to see that you are marking your answer sheet correctly, and so on. He is not there to guard you, although he will see that your competitors do not take unfair advantage. He wants to help you do your best.

2) Listen to all instructions

Don't jump the gun! Wait until you understand all directions. In most civil service tests you get more time than you need to answer the questions. So don't be in a hurry. Read each word of instructions until you clearly understand the meaning. Study the examples, listen to all announcements and follow directions. Ask questions if you do not understand what to do.

3) Identify your papers

Civil service exams are usually identified by number only. You will be assigned a number; you must not put your name on your test papers. Be sure to copy your number correctly. Since more than one exam may be given, copy your exact examination title.

4) Plan your time

Unless you are told that a test is a "speed" or "rate of work" test, speed itself is usually not important. Time enough to answer all the questions will be provided, but this does not mean that you have all day. An overall time limit has been set. Divide the total time (in minutes) by the number of questions to determine the approximate time you have for each question.

5) Do not linger over difficult questions

If you come across a difficult question, mark it with a paper clip (useful to have along) and come back to it when you have been through the booklet. One caution if you do this – be sure to skip a number on your answer sheet as well. Check often to be sure that you have not lost your place and that you are marking in the row numbered the same as the question you are answering.

6) Read the questions

Be sure you know what the question asks! Many capable people are unsuccessful because they failed to *read* the questions correctly.

7) Answer all questions

Unless you have been instructed that a penalty will be deducted for incorrect answers, it is better to guess than to omit a question.

8) Speed tests

It is often better NOT to guess on speed tests. It has been found that on timed tests people are tempted to spend the last few seconds before time is called in marking answers at random – without even reading them – in the hope of picking up a few extra points. To discourage this practice, the instructions may warn you that your score will be "corrected" for guessing. That is, a penalty will be applied. The incorrect answers will be deducted from the correct ones, or some other penalty formula will be used.

9) Review your answers

If you finish before time is called, go back to the questions you guessed or omitted to give them further thought. Review other answers if you have time.

10) Return your test materials

If you are ready to leave before others have finished or time is called, take ALL your materials to the monitor and leave quietly. Never take any test material with you. The monitor can discover whose papers are not complete, and taking a test booklet may be grounds for disqualification.

VIII. EXAMINATION TECHNIQUES

1) Read the general instructions carefully. These are usually printed on the first page of the exam booklet. As a rule, these instructions refer to the timing of the examination; the fact that you should not start work until the signal and must stop work at a signal, etc. If there are any *special* instructions, such as a choice of questions to be answered, make sure that you note this instruction carefully.

2) When you are ready to start work on the examination, that is as soon as the signal has been given, read the instructions to each question booklet, underline any key words or phrases, such as *least*, *best*, *outline*, *describe* and the like. In this way you will tend to answer as requested rather than discover on reviewing your paper that you *listed without describing*, that you selected the *worst* choice rather than the *best* choice, etc.

3) If the examination is of the objective or multiple-choice type – that is, each question will also give a series of possible answers: A, B, C or D, and you are called upon to select the best answer and write the letter next to that answer on your answer paper – it is advisable to start answering each question in turn. There may be anywhere from 50 to 100 such questions in the three or four hours allotted and you can see how much time would be taken if you read through all the questions before beginning to answer any. Furthermore, if you come across a question or group of questions which you know would be difficult to answer, it would undoubtedly affect your handling of all the other questions.

4) If the examination is of the essay type and contains but a few questions, it is a moot point as to whether you should read all the questions before starting to answer any one. Of course, if you are given a choice – say five out of seven and the like – then it is essential to read all the questions so you can eliminate the two that are most difficult. If, however, you are asked to answer all the questions, there may be danger in trying to answer the easiest one first because you may find that you will spend too much time on it. The best technique is to answer the first question, then proceed to the second, etc.

5) Time your answers. Before the exam begins, write down the time it started, then add the time allowed for the examination and write down the time it must be completed, then divide the time available somewhat as follows:

- If 3-1/2 hours are allowed, that would be 210 minutes. If you have 80 objective-type questions, that would be an average of 2-1/2 minutes per question. Allow yourself no more than 2 minutes per question, or a total of 160 minutes, which will permit about 50 minutes to review.
- If for the time allotment of 210 minutes there are 7 essay questions to answer, that would average about 30 minutes a question. Give yourself only 25 minutes per question so that you have about 35 minutes to review.

6) The most important instruction is to *read each question* and make sure you know what is wanted. The second most important instruction is to *time yourself properly* so that you answer every question. The third most important instruction is to *answer every question.* Guess if you have to but include something for each question. Remember that you will receive no credit for a blank and will probably receive some credit if you write something in answer to an essay question. If you guess a letter – say "B" for a multiple-choice question – you may have guessed right. If you leave a blank as an answer to a multiple-choice question, the examiners may respect your feelings but it will not add a point to your score. Some exams may penalize you for wrong answers, so in such cases *only*, you may not want to guess unless you have some basis for your answer.

7) Suggestions
   a. Objective-type questions
      1. Examine the question booklet for proper sequence of pages and questions
      2. Read all instructions carefully
      3. Skip any question which seems too difficult; return to it after all other questions have been answered
      4. Apportion your time properly; do not spend too much time on any single question or group of questions
      5. Note and underline key words – *all, most, fewest, least, best, worst, same, opposite,* etc.
      6. Pay particular attention to negatives
      7. Note unusual option, e.g., unduly long, short, complex, different or similar in content to the body of the question
      8. Observe the use of "hedging" words – *probably, may, most likely,* etc.
      9. Make sure that your answer is put next to the same number as the question
      10. Do not second-guess unless you have good reason to believe the second answer is definitely more correct
      11. Cross out original answer if you decide another answer is more accurate; do not erase until you are ready to hand your paper in
      12. Answer all questions; guess unless instructed otherwise
      13. Leave time for review

   b. Essay questions
      1. Read each question carefully
      2. Determine exactly what is wanted. Underline key words or phrases.
      3. Decide on outline or paragraph answer

4. Include many different points and elements unless asked to develop any one or two points or elements
5. Show impartiality by giving pros and cons unless directed to select one side only
6. Make and write down any assumptions you find necessary to answer the questions
7. Watch your English, grammar, punctuation and choice of words
8. Time your answers; don't crowd material

8) Answering the essay question

Most essay questions can be answered by framing the specific response around several key words or ideas. Here are a few such key words or ideas:

M's: manpower, materials, methods, money, management
P's: purpose, program, policy, plan, procedure, practice, problems, pitfalls, personnel, public relations

a. Six basic steps in handling problems:
    1. Preliminary plan and background development
    2. Collect information, data and facts
    3. Analyze and interpret information, data and facts
    4. Analyze and develop solutions as well as make recommendations
    5. Prepare report and sell recommendations
    6. Install recommendations and follow up effectiveness

b. Pitfalls to avoid
    1. *Taking things for granted* – A statement of the situation does not necessarily imply that each of the elements is necessarily true; for example, a complaint may be invalid and biased so that all that can be taken for granted is that a complaint has been registered
    2. *Considering only one side of a situation* – Wherever possible, indicate several alternatives and then point out the reasons you selected the best one
    3. *Failing to indicate follow up* – Whenever your answer indicates action on your part, make certain that you will take proper follow-up action to see how successful your recommendations, procedures or actions turn out to be
    4. *Taking too long in answering any single question* – Remember to time your answers properly

IX. AFTER THE TEST

Scoring procedures differ in detail among civil service jurisdictions although the general principles are the same. Whether the papers are hand-scored or graded by machine we have described, they are nearly always graded by number. That is, the person who marks the paper knows only the number – never the name – of the applicant. Not until all the papers have been graded will they be matched with names. If other tests, such as training and experience or oral interview ratings have been given, scores will be combined. Different parts of the examination usually have different weights. For example, the written test might count 60 percent of the final grade, and a rating of training and experience 40 percent. In many jurisdictions, veterans will have a certain number of points added to their grades.

After the final grade has been determined, the names are placed in grade order and an eligible list is established. There are various methods for resolving ties between those who get the same final grade – probably the most common is to place first the name of the person whose application was received first. Job offers are made from the eligible list in the order the names appear on it. You will be notified of your grade and your rank as soon as all these computations have been made. This will be done as rapidly as possible.

People who are found to meet the requirements in the announcement are called "eligibles." Their names are put on a list of eligible candidates. An eligible's chances of getting a job depend on how high he stands on this list and how fast agencies are filling jobs from the list.

When a job is to be filled from a list of eligibles, the agency asks for the names of people on the list of eligibles for that job. When the civil service commission receives this request, it sends to the agency the names of the three people highest on this list. Or, if the job to be filled has specialized requirements, the office sends the agency the names of the top three persons who meet these requirements from the general list.

The appointing officer makes a choice from among the three people whose names were sent to him. If the selected person accepts the appointment, the names of the others are put back on the list to be considered for future openings.

That is the rule in hiring from all kinds of eligible lists, whether they are for typist, carpenter, chemist, or something else. For every vacancy, the appointing officer has his choice of any one of the top three eligibles on the list. This explains why the person whose name is on top of the list sometimes does not get an appointment when some of the persons lower on the list do. If the appointing officer chooses the second or third eligible, the No. 1 eligible does not get a job at once, but stays on the list until he is appointed or the list is terminated.

X. HOW TO PASS THE INTERVIEW TEST

The examination for which you applied requires an oral interview test. You have already taken the written test and you are now being called for the interview test – the final part of the formal examination.

You may think that it is not possible to prepare for an interview test and that there are no procedures to follow during an interview. Our purpose is to point out some things you can do in advance that will help you and some good rules to follow and pitfalls to avoid while you are being interviewed.

What is an interview supposed to test?

The written examination is designed to test the technical knowledge and competence of the candidate; the oral is designed to evaluate intangible qualities, not readily measured otherwise, and to establish a list showing the relative fitness of each candidate – as measured against his competitors – for the position sought. Scoring is not on the basis of "right" and "wrong," but on a sliding scale of values ranging from "not passable" to "outstanding." As a matter of fact, it is possible to achieve a relatively low score without a single "incorrect" answer because of evident weakness in the qualities being measured.

Occasionally, an examination may consist entirely of an oral test – either an individual or a group oral. In such cases, information is sought concerning the technical knowledges and abilities of the candidate, since there has been no written examination for this purpose. More commonly, however, an oral test is used to supplement a written examination.

Who conducts interviews?

The composition of oral boards varies among different jurisdictions. In nearly all, a representative of the personnel department serves as chairman. One of the members of the board may be a representative of the department in which the candidate would work. In some cases, "outside experts" are used, and, frequently, a businessman or some other representative of the general public is asked to serve. Labor and management or other special groups may be represented. The aim is to secure the services of experts in the appropriate field.

However the board is composed, it is a good idea (and not at all improper or unethical) to ascertain in advance of the interview who the members are and what groups they represent. When you are introduced to them, you will have some idea of their backgrounds and interests, and at least you will not stutter and stammer over their names.

What should be done before the interview?

While knowledge about the board members is useful and takes some of the surprise element out of the interview, there is other preparation which is more substantive. It *is* possible to prepare for an oral interview – in several ways:

1) Keep a copy of your application and review it carefully before the interview

This may be the only document before the oral board, and the starting point of the interview. Know what education and experience you have listed there, and the sequence and dates of all of it. Sometimes the board will ask you to review the highlights of your experience for them; you should not have to hem and haw doing it.

2) Study the class specification and the examination announcement

Usually, the oral board has one or both of these to guide them. The qualities, characteristics or knowledges required by the position sought are stated in these documents. They offer valuable clues as to the nature of the oral interview. For example, if the job involves supervisory responsibilities, the announcement will usually indicate that knowledge of modern supervisory methods and the qualifications of the candidate as a supervisor will be tested. If so, you can expect such questions, frequently in the form of a hypothetical situation which you are expected to solve. NEVER go into an oral without knowledge of the duties and responsibilities of the job you seek.

3) Think through each qualification required

Try to visualize the kind of questions you would ask if you were a board member. How well could you answer them? Try especially to appraise your own knowledge and background in each area, *measured against the job sought*, and identify any areas in which you are weak. Be critical and realistic – do not flatter yourself.

4) Do some general reading in areas in which you feel you may be weak

For example, if the job involves supervision and your past experience has NOT, some general reading in supervisory methods and practices, particularly in the field of human relations, might be useful. Do NOT study agency procedures or detailed manuals. The oral board will be testing your understanding and capacity, not your memory.

5) Get a good night's sleep and watch your general health and mental attitude

You will want a clear head at the interview. Take care of a cold or any other minor ailment, and of course, no hangovers.

What should be done on the day of the interview?

Now comes the day of the interview itself. Give yourself plenty of time to get there. Plan to arrive somewhat ahead of the scheduled time, particularly if your appointment is in the fore part of the day. If a previous candidate fails to appear, the board might be ready for you a bit early. By early afternoon an oral board is almost invariably behind schedule if there are many candidates, and you may have to wait. Take along a book or magazine to read, or your application to review, but leave any extraneous material in the waiting room when you go in for your interview. In any event, relax and compose yourself.

The matter of dress is important. The board is forming impressions about you – from your experience, your manners, your attitude, and your appearance. Give your personal appearance careful attention. Dress your best, but not your flashiest. Choose conservative, appropriate clothing, and be sure it is immaculate. This is a business interview, and your appearance should indicate that you regard it as such. Besides, being well groomed and properly dressed will help boost your confidence.

Sooner or later, someone will call your name and escort you into the interview room. *This is it.* From here on you are on your own. It is too late for any more preparation. But remember, you asked for this opportunity to prove your fitness, and you are here because your request was granted.

What happens when you go in?

The usual sequence of events will be as follows: The clerk (who is often the board stenographer) will introduce you to the chairman of the oral board, who will introduce you to the other members of the board. Acknowledge the introductions before you sit down. Do not be surprised if you find a microphone facing you or a stenotypist sitting by. Oral interviews are usually recorded in the event of an appeal or other review.

Usually the chairman of the board will open the interview by reviewing the highlights of your education and work experience from your application – primarily for the benefit of the other members of the board, as well as to get the material into the record. Do not interrupt or comment unless there is an error or significant misinterpretation; if that is the case, do not hesitate. But do not quibble about insignificant matters. Also, he will usually ask you some question about your education, experience or your present job – partly to get you to start talking and to establish the interviewing "rapport." He may start the actual questioning, or turn it over to one of the other members. Frequently, each member undertakes the questioning on a particular area, one in which he is perhaps most competent, so you can expect each member to participate in the examination. Because time is limited, you may also expect some rather abrupt switches in the direction the questioning takes, so do not be upset by it. Normally, a board member will not pursue a single line of questioning unless he discovers a particular strength or weakness.

After each member has participated, the chairman will usually ask whether any member has any further questions, then will ask you if you have anything you wish to add. Unless you are expecting this question, it may floor you. Worse, it may start you off on an extended, extemporaneous speech. The board is not usually seeking more information. The question is principally to offer you a last opportunity to present further qualifications or to indicate that you have nothing to add. So, if you feel that a significant qualification or characteristic has been overlooked, it is proper to point it out in a sentence or so. Do not compliment the board on the thoroughness of their examination – they have been sketchy, and you know it. If you wish, merely say, "No thank you, I have nothing further to add." This is a point where you can "talk yourself out" of a good impression or fail to present an important bit of information. Remember, *you close the interview yourself.*

The chairman will then say, "That is all, Mr. ______, thank you." Do not be startled; the interview is over, and quicker than you think. Thank him, gather your belongings and take your leave. Save your sigh of relief for the other side of the door.

How to put your best foot forward

Throughout this entire process, you may feel that the board individually and collectively is trying to pierce your defenses, seek out your hidden weaknesses and embarrass and confuse you. Actually, this is not true. They are obliged to make an appraisal of your qualifications for the job you are seeking, and they want to see you in your best light. Remember, they must interview all candidates and a non-cooperative candidate may become a failure in spite of their best efforts to bring out his qualifications. Here are 15 suggestions that will help you:

1) Be natural – Keep your attitude confident, not cocky

If you are not confident that you can do the job, do not expect the board to be. Do not apologize for your weaknesses, try to bring out your strong points. The board is interested in a positive, not negative, presentation. Cockiness will antagonize any board member and make him wonder if you are covering up a weakness by a false show of strength.

2) Get comfortable, but don't lounge or sprawl

Sit erectly but not stiffly. A careless posture may lead the board to conclude that you are careless in other things, or at least that you are not impressed by the importance of the occasion. Either conclusion is natural, even if incorrect. Do not fuss with your clothing, a pencil or an ashtray. Your hands may occasionally be useful to emphasize a point; do not let them become a point of distraction.

3) Do not wisecrack or make small talk

This is a serious situation, and your attitude should show that you consider it as such. Further, the time of the board is limited – they do not want to waste it, and neither should you.

4) Do not exaggerate your experience or abilities

In the first place, from information in the application or other interviews and sources, the board may know more about you than you think. Secondly, you probably will not get away with it. An experienced board is rather adept at spotting such a situation, so do not take the chance.

5) If you know a board member, do not make a point of it, yet do not hide it

Certainly you are not fooling him, and probably not the other members of the board. Do not try to take advantage of your acquaintanceship – it will probably do you little good.

6) Do not dominate the interview

Let the board do that. They will give you the clues – do not assume that you have to do all the talking. Realize that the board has a number of questions to ask you, and do not try to take up all the interview time by showing off your extensive knowledge of the answer to the first one.

7) Be attentive

You only have 20 minutes or so, and you should keep your attention at its sharpest throughout. When a member is addressing a problem or question to you, give him your undivided attention. Address your reply principally to him, but do not exclude the other board members.

8) Do not interrupt

A board member may be stating a problem for you to analyze. He will ask you a question when the time comes. Let him state the problem, and wait for the question.

9) Make sure you understand the question

Do not try to answer until you are sure what the question is. If it is not clear, restate it in your own words or ask the board member to clarify it for you. However, do not haggle about minor elements.

10) Reply promptly but not hastily

A common entry on oral board rating sheets is "candidate responded readily," or "candidate hesitated in replies." Respond as promptly and quickly as you can, but do not jump to a hasty, ill-considered answer.

11) Do not be peremptory in your answers

A brief answer is proper – but do not fire your answer back. That is a losing game from your point of view. The board member can probably ask questions much faster than you can answer them.

12) Do not try to create the answer you think the board member wants

He is interested in what kind of mind you have and how it works – not in playing games. Furthermore, he can usually spot this practice and will actually grade you down on it.

13) Do not switch sides in your reply merely to agree with a board member

Frequently, a member will take a contrary position merely to draw you out and to see if you are willing and able to defend your point of view. Do not start a debate, yet do not surrender a good position. If a position is worth taking, it is worth defending.

14) Do not be afraid to admit an error in judgment if you are shown to be wrong

The board knows that you are forced to reply without any opportunity for careful consideration. Your answer may be demonstrably wrong. If so, admit it and get on with the interview.

15) Do not dwell at length on your present job

The opening question may relate to your present assignment. Answer the question but do not go into an extended discussion. You are being examined for a *new* job, not your present one. As a matter of fact, try to phrase ALL your answers in terms of the job for which you are being examined.

Basis of Rating

Probably you will forget most of these "do's" and "don'ts" when you walk into the oral interview room. Even remembering them all will not ensure you a passing grade. Perhaps you did not have the qualifications in the first place. But remembering them will help you to put your best foot forward, without treading on the toes of the board members.

Rumor and popular opinion to the contrary notwithstanding, an oral board wants you to make the best appearance possible. They know you are under pressure – but they also want to see how you respond to it as a guide to what your reaction would be under the pressures of the job you seek. They will be influenced by the degree of poise you display, the personal traits you show and the manner in which you respond.

ABOUT THIS BOOK

This book contains tests divided into Examination Sections. Go through each test, answering every question in the margin. At the end of each test look at the answer key and check your answers. On the ones you got wrong, look at the right answer choice and learn. Do not fill in the answers first. Do not memorize the questions and answers, but understand the answer and principles involved. On your test, the questions will likely be different from the samples. Questions are changed and new ones added. If you understand these past questions you should have success with any changes that arise. Tests may consist of several types of questions. We have additional books on each subject should more study be advisable or necessary for you. Finally, the more you study, the better prepared you will be. This book is intended to be the last thing you study before you walk into the examination room. Prior study of relevant texts is also recommended. NLC publishes some of these in our Fundamental Series. Knowledge and good sense are important factors in passing your exam. Good luck also helps. So now study this Passbook, absorb the material contained within and take that knowledge into the examination. Then do your best to pass that exam.

EXAMINATION SECTION

EXAMINATION SECTION
TEST 1

DIRECTIONS: Each question or incomplete statement is followed by several suggested answers or completions. Select the one that BEST answers the question or completes the statement. *PRINT THE LETTER OF THE CORRECT ANSWER IN THE SPACE AT THE RIGHT.*

1. Which of following can usually NOT be accomplished through the use of an accounting system? 1.____

   A. Providing information to managers, owners, and other parties about solvency
   B. Recording financial activity in monetary terms
   C. Assuring profitability
   D. Summarizing financial activities in a way that is useful

2. The main difference between financial accounting and managerial accounting is that financial accounting 2.____

   A. must be performed by a CPA
   B. is performed for the purposes of internal control and oversight
   C. is required by law
   D. focuses on the information needs of external parties

3. Curry Landscaping purchased a concrete mixer with an invoice price of $8000. The terms of sale were 2/10. n/30, and Curry Landscaping paid within the discount period. Curry also paid a $100 delivery charge, a $130 installment charge, and $550 sales tax. What amount would be recorded as the cost of the equipment? 3.____

   A. $8250
   B. $8390
   C. $8620
   D. $8780

4. In the ______ method for reporting cash used in operating activities, the accountant lists the major classes of gross cash receipts and the gross cash payments from operations. 4.____

   A. double-entry
   B. indirect
   C. work sheet
   D. direct

5. Unearned revenue is a(n) 5.____

   A. expense
   B. revenue
   C. liability
   D. asset

6. A debit is used to record a decrease in a(n) 6.____

   I. asset
   II. liability
   III. owners' equity
   IV. expense

   A. I only
   B. I and III
   C. II, III and IV
   D. I, II, III and IV

7. During its month's-end procedures at the end of July, the Blue Tang Inn neglects to include the adjusting entry to recognize interest owed to a lender. As a result, the 7.____

   A. expenses are understated and July 31 owners' equity understated
   B. expenses are understated and July 31 assets overstated
   C. net income is understated and July 31 assets overstated
   D. net income is overstated and July 31 liabilities understated

8. The ______ method is used to classify individual receivables according to time elapsed from their due date. 8.____

   A. pro rata
   B. aging
   C. allowance
   D. direct write-off

9. Credit is given on terms 2/10, n/30. This means that there will be a 9.____

   A. 2% cash discount if the amount is paid within 10 days, with the balance due in 30 days
   B. 10% cash discount if the amount is paid within 2 days, with the balance due in 30 days
   C. 30% discount if paid within 2 days
   D. 30% discount if paid within 10 days

10. Which of the following accounts normally has a credit balance? 10.____

   A. Office equipment
   B. Sales salaries expense
   C. Sales salaries payable
   D. Cash

11. Revenue earned on an account results in 11.____

   A. an increase in that asset, but a decrease in another asset
   B. decreased assets and increased owners' equity
   C. increased assets and increased owners' equity
   D. decreased assets and decreased owners' equity

Questions 12-14 are based on the following information: Montana Ned's Golf Supply, at the end of last year, had merchandise costing $210,000 in inventory. During January of the current year, Montana Ned's bought merchandise costing $93,000, and sold merchandise for which it had paid a total of $81,000. Montana Ned's uses a perpetual inventory system.

12. What is the balance in the inventory account on January 31? 12.____

A. $93,000
B. $210,000
C. $222,000
D. $384,000

13. What was the amount of costs transferred to from the inventory account to the cost of goods sold account during January? 13.____

A. $12,000
B. $81,000
C. $93,000
D. $174,000

14. What was the total debited to Montana Ned's inventory account in January? 14.____

A. $12,000
B. $81,000
C. $93,000
D. $174,000

15. Which of the following is TRUE about restrictions on retained earnings? 15.____

A. They do not change overall retained earnings.
B. They increase overall retained earnings.
C. They decrease overall retained earnings.
D. They provide a cash fund for contingencies.

16. A(n) ______ discount is a deduction from the invoice price of goods allowed if payment is made within a specified period of time. 16.____

A. trade
B. early-bird
C. bulk
D. cash

17. A promissory note received from a customer in exchange for an account receivable would be classified as a(n) ______ for the recipient 17.____

A. note payable
B. account receivable
C. cash equivalent
D. note receivable

18. The balance of an unearned revenue account appears in 18.____

A. a separate section of the income statement for revenue not yet earned
B. the liability section of the balance sheet
C. the income statement along with other revenue accounts
D. the balance sheet as a component of owners' equity

19. The maximum number of years a company is allowed to record a single intangible asset is 19.____

A. 10
B. 17
C. 20
D. 35

20. Notes payable typically appear on the 20.____

A. income statement
B. balance sheet
C. statement of cash flows
D. statement of retained earnings

21. The most likely reason why a corporation's stock trades at a very high price/earnings ratio is that 21.____

A. the corporation has several classes of stock outstanding
B. the corporation is very large and considered a low risk
C. investors expect the corporation to have higher earnings in the future
D. investors intend to sell short

22. World Water has total current liabilities of $70,000. After employees are paid $10,000 of the wages payable to the company owed from last year, current liabilities would be 22.____

A. $60,000
B. $70,000
C. $75,000
D. $80,000

23. Which of the following is included in a company's cash flow from financing activities? 23.____

A. Cash received from the issue of common stock
B. Cash paid for employee salaries
C. Cash paid for income taxes
D. Cash paid for the purchase of capital equipment

24. Which of the following is a current liability? 24.____

A. Buildings used in business operations
B. Wages payable
C. Office supplies
D. Long-term note payable

25. An end-of-period inventory amount that is incorrectly reported can result in misstated 25.____

I. net income
II. gross profits
III. current assets
IV. cost of goods sold

A. I and II
B. I, II and III
C. III and IV
D. I, II, III and IV

KEY (CORRECT ANSWERS)

1. C
2. D
3. C
4. D
5. C
6. C
7. D
8. B
9. A
10. C
11. C
12. C
13. B
14. C
15. A
16. D
17. D
18. B
19. C
20. B
21. C
22. A
23. A
24. B
25. D

TEST 2

DIRECTIONS: Each question or incomplete statement is followed by several suggested answers or completions. Select the one that BEST answers the question or completes the statement. *PRINT THE LETTER OF THE CORRECT ANSWER IN THE SPACE AT THE RIGHT.*

1. Sales for the year were $200,000, and the cost of sales was $ 120,000. If the average inventory for the year was $40,000, what was the inventory turnover? 1.____

   A. 1.67
   B. 3
   C. 3.67
   D. 5

2. Chuzzlewit Enterprises sold equipment for $30,000. The cost was $70,000, and the equipment had accumulated depreciation of $50,000 at the time of the sale. If the is using the direct method, the amount of ______ would be entered for this transaction in the operating section of the cash flow statement. 2.____

   A. $(10,000)
   B. 0 (no entry)
   C. $10,000
   D. $30,000

3. An accountant is preparing a bank reconciliation. A service charge shown on the bank statement should be 3.____

   A. deducted from the balance in the depositor's records
   B. deducted from the balance in the bank statement
   C. added to the balance in the depositor's records
   D. added to the balance in the depositor's records

4. For several years, the net income of Stanton, Inc. has been rising as a percentage of the company's net sales. Analysts would usually interpret this to mean that 4.____

   A. the portion of the company's assets that are financed on credit is decreasing
   B. net sales are increasing faster than inflation
   C. sales volume has been decreasing
   D. the company has been successfully controlling expenses

5. Which of the following occurs when a company issues a stock dividend? 5.____

   A. Earned capital increases and contributed capital decreases.
   B. Earned capital decreases and contributed capital increases.
   C. Total shareholder equity increases.
   D. Total shareholder equity decreases.

6. Harlan uses a perpetual inventory system. Its beginning inventory for the current year was 10 units, purchased at a cost of $10 each. During the current year Harlan purchased 20 units at $12 each. 12 units are sold in the current year. Using the first-in, first-out (FIFO) method, calculate the total cost of the 12 units that were sold. 6.____

A. $116
B. $120
C. $124
D. $130

7. Bad debt expense can be estimated by using the _______ method. 7.____

I. percent of accounts receivable
II. percent of sales
III. allowance
IV. aging of accounts receivable

A. I only
B. I and II
C. III only
D. I, II, III and IV

8. Accelerated methods of depreciation include the _______ method. 8.____

I. sum-of-the-years'-digits
II. double declining balance
III. production units
IV. straight-line

A. I and II
B. II and III
C. I, III and IV
D. I, II, III and IV

Questions 9 and 10 refer to the following: Bougainville Enterprises reports the following resu'ts in its financial statements.

	2018	2017	2016
Net Sales	$2.5 million	$2.05 million	$1.9 million
Accounts Receivable, ending	$175,000	$167,000	$165,000

9. For 2017, Bougainville's accounts receivable turnover rate was 9.____

A. 12.3
B. 14.6
C. 16.5
D. 17.8

10. For 2018, Bougainville's accounts receivable turnover rate was 10.____

A. 12.3
B. 14.6
C. 16.5
D. 17.8

11. Cash equivalents include 11.____

A. money orders
B. 6-month certificates of deposit

C. checking accounts
D. short-term liquid investments

12. Rent expense typically appears on the 12.____

A. income statement
B. statement of retained earnings
C. statement of cash flows
D. balance sheet

13. Hexagon Corporation has 1,000 shares of $100 par value preferred stock, and $25,000 shares of common stock outstanding. Its total stockholders' equity is $500,000. The book value per common share is 13.____

A. $15
B. $16
C. $18.25
D. $20

14. Which of the following items would NOT be added to the balance per book? 14.____

A. A deposit in transit
B. A customer note collected by the bank
C. Interest earned on an account
D. A check for $100 recorded as $ 100 in the check register

15. The ______ ratio is a type of profitability ratio. 15.____

A. current
B. quick
C. accounts receivable turnover
D. return on assets

16. The concept of adequate disclosure means that financial statements should be accompanied by an information for the statements to be interpreted properly. Examples of these notations include 16.____

I. due dates of major liabilities
II. accounting methods and policies
III. significant events occurring between the time the balance sheet was recorded and the financial statements were issued
IV. name of the company's financial institution

A. I and II
B. I, II and III
C. III only
D. I, II, III and IV

17. What is the term used to describe horizontal addition or subtraction across columns? 17.____

A. Cross-footing
B. Keying
C. Journalizing
D. Footing

18. The ______ method is recommended for amortization of discounts or premiums. 18.____

    A. double declining balance
    B. straight-line
    C. effective interest
    D. sum-of-the-years' -digits

19. Each of the following is a quick asset, EXCEPT 19.____

    A. current receivables
    B. cash
    C. short-term investments
    D. inventory

20. Mo-Kan Corporation issued 6,000 shares of its $ 10 par value common stock in exchange for land that has a market value of $48,000. The entry to record this transaction would include a 20.____

    A. $60,000 debit to common stock
    B. $84,000 credit to common stock
    C. $24,000 credit to contributed capital in excess of par value, CS
    D. $60,000 debit to land

21. An accountant has analyzed a company's transactions and recorded them in a journal. The next step in the accounting cycle is 21.____

    A. posting
    B. preparing the financial statements
    C. preparing an unadjusted trial balance
    D. closing temporary accounts

22. At the end of the year, before adjusting and closing accounts had been done, the allowance for doubtful accounts of Blue Lilith showed a credit balance of $300. An aging of the accounts receivable indicated an amount of $3900 to be probably uncollectible. Given these circumstances, a year-end adjusting entry for bad debts expense would include a ______ credit to the allowance for doubtful accounts. 22.____

    A. $360
    B. $3600
    C. $3900
    D. $4200

23. Junan Corporation purchased a machine that had an estimated useful life of 5 years. After the machine had been operating for 3 years, however, it is determined that the original estimate should have been 10 years. At the time this determination was made, the remaining cost to be depreciated should be allocated over the subsequent ______ years. 23.____

    A. 3
    B. 5
    C. 7
    D. 10

24. During the current year, Hastings Corporation made the purchases shown below: 24.

January	10 units@$ 120
February	20 units@$ 130
April	15 units@$ 140
August	12 units@$150
October	10 units@$ 160

At the end of the year, Hastings had 26 units remaining in ending inventory, consisting of 2 from January, 4 from February, 6 from April, 4 from August, and 10 from October. Using the specific identification method, calculate the cost of ending inventory.

A. $3500
B. $3800
C. $3920
D. $3960

25. Advantages associated with bond financing include 25.____

I. no change in ownership's degree of control
II. tax-deductible interest
III. the ability to trade on equity
IV. guaranteed return on equity

A. I and II
B. I, II and III
C. II, III and IV
D. I, II, III and IV

KEY (CORRECT ANSWERS)

1. B
2. B
3. A
4. D
5. B
6. C
7. D
8. A
9. A
10. B
11. D
12. A
13. B
14. A
15. D
16. B
17. A
18. C
19. D
20. C
21. A
22. B
23. C
24. B
25. B

TEST 3

DIRECTIONS: Each question or incomplete statement is followed by several suggested answers or completions. Select the one that BEST answers the question or completes the statement. *PRINT THE LETTER OF THE CORRECT ANSWER IN THE SPACE AT THE RIGHT.*

1. _______ stock is a term that refers to shares of a corporation's stock that have been issued and reacquired, but not canceled. 1.____

   A. Cumulative preferred
   B. No-par
   C. Non-cumulative preferred
   D. Treasury

2. The paid-in capital section of a balance sheet includes each of the following, EXCEPT 2.____

   A. retained earnings
   B. preferred stock
   C. common stock
   D. common stock subscribed

3. Chubby Taxi just purchased a new cab. The initial cost would include each of the following, EXCEPT 3.____

   A. sales tax
   B. purchase price
   C. the installation of air conditioning before using the cab
   D. first year's liability insurance

4. During a period of rising costs, the _______ method of inventory valuation method yields the lowest reported net income. 4.____

   A. last in, first out (LIFO)
   B. first in, first out (FIFO)
   C. weighted-average
   D. average cost

5. Unearned revenues are 5.____

   A. any increases to owners' equity
   B. revenues that have been earned and received, but not deposited
   C. revenues that have been earned, but not yet collected
   D. liabilities that are created by advance payments for goods or services

6. Red Max Corporation had a credit balance in the allowance for doubtful accounts of $200 at the start of the current year. During the year, a provision of 2% of sales was made for uncollectible accounts. Sales for the year were $500,000 and $8000 of accounts receivable were written off as worthless. Also, no recoveries of accounts previously written off were made during the year. The year-end financial statement would show a 6.____

   A. $ 10,000 credit balance in the allowance for doubtful accounts
   B. $2000 credit balance in the allowance for doubtful accounts
   C. $ 10,200 bad debts expense

D. $9800 bad debts expense

7. A company's current assets include 7.____
   I. Merchandise inventory
   II. Prepaid expenses
   III. Accounts receivable
   IV. Land held for future plant expansion

   A. I and II
   B. II and III
   C. I, II, and III
   D. I, II, III and IV

8. The maturity value of a note is the 8.____

   A. face value plus any stated interest
   B. discounted value of the note
   C. par value less the discount
   D. principal less the discount

9. A company can retire bonds by 9.____
   I. converting them to stock for the holders
   II. paying off the bonds at maturity.
   III. purchasing the bonds on the open market
   IV. exercising a call option

   A. I and II
   B. II and III
   C. III only
   D. I, II, III and IV

10. Within the past year, Wildcat Oil purchased and then sold land containing 15 million gallons of oil for $4,875,000. While it owned the land, Wildcat pumped and sold 789,000 gallons of oil. The depletion expense for the year would be 10.____

    A. $97,500
    B. $181,995
    C. $256,425
    D. $301,667

11. Genetico has sold land for cash at a price greater than its cost. Each of the following is a result of this transaction, EXCEPT that 11.____

    A. owners' equity is increased
    B. total assets are unaffected
    C. cash is increased
    D. liabilities are unaffected

12. Which of the following is a financing activity? 12.____

    A. Signing a note payable in exchange for cash
    B. Settling an account payable with cash
    C. Purchasing a warehouse in exchange for shares of stock
    D. Selling land for cash

13. The Kasnoff Group adjusts its accounts at the end of the year for consulting services of $9000 performed for a client in December that have not yet been collected in cash. This adjustment will result in a $9000 13.____

    A. decrease in both liabilities and owners' equity
    B. increase in both assets and liabilities
    C. increase in both assets and owners' equity
    D. decrease in both assets and liabilities

14. Which of the following would be recorded as a contingent liability? 14.____

    A. Debt guarantees
    B. Warranty on products sold
    C. Unearned revenues
    D. Properly taxes payable

15. "Mark to market' is the balance sheet valuation standard for 15.____

    A. investments in capital stock of any corporation
    B. stockholders' equity of any publicly traded corporation
    C. investments in all financial assets
    D. investments in marketable securities

16. Frogpond Enterprises normally sells it product for $20 each, which involves a profit margin of 25%. The selling price has fallen to $15. Frog-pond's current inventory is 200 units, purchased at $16 each. Replacement cost is not $13 per unit. Using the lower of cost or market, Frogpond's inventory is now valued at 16.____

    A. $2500
    B. $2550
    C. $2600
    D. $2700

17. According to the concept of present value, a bond that paid a below market rate would sell at a price 17.____

    A. below its maturity value
    B. equal to its maturity value
    C. above its maturity value
    D. that may vary in accordance with the issuer's credit rating

Questions 18-20 are based on the following information: Aquitaine's stockholders earn $6 per share and $2 dividends annually on stocks that are priced at $24 per share. The common shareholders' equity is $600,000, and the shares of common stock outstanding amount to $1.2 million.

18. Aquitaine's P/E ratio is 18.____

    A. 0.33
    B. 2
    C. 3
    D. 4

19. Aquitaine's dividend yield is 19.____

A. 0.083
B. 0.33
C. 1.2
D. 3

20. The book value per share of Aquitaine stock is 20.____

A. 0.25
B. 0.5
C. 2
D. 4

21. Which of the following would cause a temporary difference between taxable and pretax accounting income? 21.____

A. Life insurance benefits paid upon the death of an executive officer
B. Investment expenses incurred to generate tax-exempt income
C. The deduction of dividends received
D. The use of MACRS to depreciate equipment

22. If a bond has a par value of $ 1000 and the market price is $989.10, the bond is selling at 22.____

A. a discount
B. the coupon rate
C. a premium
D. face value

23. If revenues are less than expenses during a given accounting period, 23.____

I. the income statement will show a net loss
II. assets will decrease more than liabilities
III. owners' equity will decrease more than assets
IV. the cash account will decrease

A. I only
B. I and II
C. I, II, and III
D. I, II, III and IV

24. Klaxor receives a 10%, 90-day note for $1500. The total interest on the note is 24.____

A. $37.50
B. $50
C. $75
D. $87.50

25. STX International and Holoport each makes and sells telecommunications equipment. Holoport uses the first-in, first-out (FIFO) method for valuing inventory, and STX uses last-in, first-out (FIFO). Due to technological innovations and improvements, the cost of making telecommunications equipment has decreased-over the past several years. Based on these assumptions, STX International-over the past several years-would be more likely to 25.____

A. have a lower inventory value on the year-end balance sheet
B. report a higher gross margin on the income statement
C. have a higher amount of owners' equity
D. pay less in income taxes

KEY (CORRECT ANSWERS)

1. D
2. A
3. D
4. A
5. D

6. B
7. C
8. A
9. D
10. C

11. B
12. A
13. C
14. A
15. D

16. C
17. A
18. D
19. A
20. B

21. D
22. A
23. A
24. A
25. C

TEST 4

DIRECTIONS: Each question or incomplete statement is followed by several suggested answers or completions. Select the one that BEST answers the question or completes the statement. *PRINT THE LETTER OF THE CORRECT ANSWER IN THE SPACE AT THE RIGHT.*

1. Which of the following is NOT a short-term liquidity ratio? 1.____

   A. Defensive interval
   B. Inventory turnover
   C. Accounts receivable turnover
   D. Debt to total assets

2. What is the term for the original cost of an asset less its accumulated depreciation? 2.____

   A. Net present value
   B. Replacement cost
   C. Current value
   D. Book value

3. Starlingcourt, which has total assets of $400,000, borrows $80,000 from the bank. Which of the following is true? 3.____

   A. Owners' equity remains unchanged.
   B. Owners' equity increases by $80,000.
   C. Owners' equity decreases by $80,000.
   D. Total assets are now $320,000.

4. Of the following steps in the accounting cycle, which is performed the LATEST in the process? 4.____

   A. Adjusting accounts
   B. Preparing financial statements
   C. Preparing the adjusted trial balance
   D. Posting

5. When a business pays a liability with cash, the accountant should record the decrease in 5.____

   A. cash as a debit
   B. accounts receivable as a credit
   C. accounts receivable as a debit
   D. accounts payable as a debit

6. Bettancourt issues 9%, 20-year bonds with a par value of $750,000. The current market rate is 9%. The total amount of interest owed to bondholders for each semiannual interest payment is 6.____

   A. $33,750
   B. $67,500
   C. $101,250
   D. $135,000

7. The statement of cash flows helps in the analysis of the 7.____
   I. differences between net income and net operating cash flow
   II. means used to finance investing activities
   III. source of cash for debt repayment
   IV. source of cash for plant expansion

   A. I and II
   B. II and III
   C. III only
   D. I, II, III and IV

8. A company's quick ratio is 8.____

   A. in indication of the time a company takes to pay its short-term creditors
   B. never larger than its current ratio on the same day
   C. determined by dividing current assets by current liabilities, excluding accounts payable for inventory purchases
   D. an indication of how quickly a company converts its current assets to cash.

9. Hazbin Corporation has assets of $100,000, liabilities of $ 10,000, and equity of $90,000. It buys office equipment on credit for $5,000. Effects of this transaction include a 9.____
   I. $5000 increase in liabilities
   II. $5000 increase in assets
   III. $5000 increase in equity
   IV. $5000 decrease in equity

   A. I only
   B. I and II
   C. I, II and III
   D. IV only

10. Pet Palace used the retail method to estimate its ending inventory in its monthly financial statements. On November 30, goods available for sale during the month had cost $20,000 and had been given retail prices of $50,000. Sales for the month amounted to $30,000. The estimated ending inventory to appear in the November 30 balance sheet is 10.____

    A. $8000
    B. $12,000
    C. $20,000
    D. $38,000

11. The double-entry system of accounting requires that 11.____

    A. the total number of debit entries must equal the number of credit entries
    B. debits must equal credits when the trial balance is prepared
    C. two entries must be made for each transaction
    D. the dollar amount of debit items must equal the dollar amount of credit items for each journal entry

Questions 12-14 refer to the information below.
Ukraine Appliance Outlet uses a periodic inventory system. It sold 900 kitchen mixers in the last year. The inventory data was as follows:

1/1	Balance	100 mixers@ $70.00	=$ 7000
3/6	Bought	500 mixers@ $80.00	=$40,000
7/15	Bought	400 mixers@ $90.00	=$36,000
10/23	Bought	400 mixers@ $100.00	=$40.000
Inventory available:		1400 mixers	$123,000

12. Under the first-in, first-out (FIFO) method, ending inventory is 12.____

A. $35,000
B. $39,000
C. $49,000
D. $50,000

13. Under the last-in, last-out (LIFO) method, ending inventory is 13.____

A. $35,000
B. $39,000
C. $49,000
D. $50,000

14. Cost of goods sold under the last-in, last-out (LIFO) method is 14.____

A. $71,000
B. $74,000
C. $84,000
D. $87,000

15. A company that sold machinery during an accounting period would record the transaction as a(n) 15.____

A. financing activity inflow
B. financing activity outflow
C. investing activity inflow
D. investing activity outflow

16. Ugolino Enterprises had net sales of $4.235 billion and ending accounts receivable of $775 million, resulting in ______ days' sales uncol- lected. 16.____

A. 34.7
B. 65.2
C. 66.8
D. 81.8

17. The ______ principle requires that financial statement information be based on costs incurred in business transactions, and requires assets and services to be recorded initially at the cash or cash-equivalent amount given in exchange. 17.____

A. cost
B. business entity
C. going-concern
D. realization

18. Carlson Corporation earns a rate of return on common stockholders' equity of 14%. The company will cause the rate of return to increase if it 18.____

    A. increases its P/E ratio
    B. increases the size of the cash dividend paid on common stock
    C. increases the market price of its stock
    D. issues 10% bonds and invests the proceeds to earn 12%

19. An adjusting entry for accrued revenues will increase the ______ account. 19.____

    I. revenue
    II. expense
    III. asset
    IV. liability

    A. I only
    B. I and III
    C. II and IV
    D. IV only

20. Which of the following would be recorded as an estimated liability? 20.____

    A. Accounts payable
    B. Payroll taxes payable
    C. Income taxes payable
    D. Lawsuit against the company

21. Stabile Corporation has the following information available at year's end: 21.____

Cost of Goods Sold	$175,000
Net Credit Sales	$250,000
Beginning inventory	$40,000
Beginning accounts receivable	$15,000
Ending inventory	$50,000
Ending accounts receivable	$45,000

Stabile's inventory turnover ratio for the year was

    A. 0.31
    B. 3.5
    C. 3.89
    D. 5.21

22. Liquidating dividends are distributed when 22.____

    A. a company pays dividends in excess of its retained earnings
    B. the company is extremely profitable
    C. the dividends are in arrears
    D. there are both common and preferred dividends

23. The gross margin method of estimating ending inventory 23.____

    A. is the most accurate estimating method
    B. uses the current relationship between goods available for sale and retail prices

C. uses the historical average gross margin percent
D. uses only the most recent gross margin percent

24. Hafkemeyer Irrigation, which uses a perpetual inventory system, had a beginning inventory of 5 units, costing $20 each. During the year it made two purchases: the first for 10 units at $22 each and the second for 6 units at $25 each. 8 units were sold for $350 retail. Using the last-in, first-out (LIFO) method, calculate the value of the inventory after these 8 sales were made. 24.____

A. $276
B. $288
C. $296
D. $304

25. Cash includes 25.____

I. deposits in checking and savings accounts
II. any item that a bank customarily accepts for immediate deposit
III. IOUs
IV. notes receivable

A. I only
B. I and II
C. I, II and III
D. I, II, III and IV

KEY (CORRECT ANSWERS)

1.	D	11.	D
2.	D	12.	C
3.	A	13.	B
4.	B	14.	C
5.	D	15.	C
6.	A	16.	C
7.	D	17.	A
8.	B	18.	D
9.	B	19.	B
10.	A	20.	C

21. C
22. A
23. C
24. C
25. B

EXAMINATION SECTION

TEST 1

DIRECTIONS: Each question or incomplete statement is followed by several suggested answers or completions. Select the one that BEST answers the question or completes the statement. *PRINT THE LETTER OF THE CORRECT ANSWER IN THE SPACE AT THE RIGHT.*

1. The independent auditor's PRIMARY objective in reviewing internal control is to provide 1.____
   A. assurance of the client's operational efficiency
   B. a basis for reliance on the system and determination of the scope of the auditing procedures
   C. a basis for suggestions for improving the client's accounting system
   D. evidence of the client's adherence to prescribed managerial policies

2. If there is an increase in work-in-process inventory during a period, 2.____
   A. cost of goods sold will be greater than cost of goods manufactured
   B. cost of goods manufactured will be greater than cost of goods sold
   C. manufacturing costs (production costs) for the period will be greater than cost of goods manufactured
   D. manufacturing costs for the period will be less than cost of goods manufactured

Questions 3-4.

DIRECTIONS: Questions 3 and 4 are to be answered on the basis of the information given below about the Parr Company and the Farr Company.

The Parr Company purchased 800 of the 1,000 outstanding shares of the Farr Company's common stock for $80,000 on January 1, 2021. During 2021, the Farr Company declared dividends of $8,000 and reported earnings for the year of $20,000.

3. Using the equity method, the investment in Farr Company on the Parr Company's books should show a balance, at December 31, 2021, of 3.____
   A. $89,600 B. $$86,400 C. $80,000 D. $73,600

4. If, instead of using the equity method, the Parr Company uses the cost method, the balance, at December 31, 2021, in the investment account, should be 4.____
   A. $96,000 B. $86,400 C. $80,000 D. $73,600

Questions 5-6.

DIRECTIONS: Questions 5 and 6 are to be answered on the basis of the information given below about the Fame Corporation.

The Fame Corporation has 50,000 shares of $10 par value common stock authorized, issued, and outstanding. The 50,000 shares were issued at $12 per share. The retained earnings of the company are $60,000.

5. Assuming that the Fame Corporation reacquired 1,000 of its common shares at $15 per share and the par value method of accounting for treasury stock was used, the result would be that — 5.____
   A. stockholders' equity would increase by $15,000
   B. capital in excess of par would decrease by at least $2,000
   C. retained earnings would decrease by $5,000
   D. common stock would decrease by at least $15,000

6. Assuming that the Fame Corporation reissued 1,000 of its common shares at $11 per share and the cost method of accounting for treasury stock was used, the result would be that — 6.____
   A. book value per share of common stock would decrease
   B. retained earnings would decrease by $11,000
   C. donated surplus would be credited for $5,500
   D. a gain on reissue of treasury stock account would be charged

7. On January 31, 2012, when the Montana Corporation's stock was selling at $36 per share, its capital accounts were as follows: — 7.____

Capital Stock (par value $20; 100,000 shares issued)	$2,000,000
Premium on Capital Stock	800,000
Retained Earnings	4,550,000

   If the corporation declares a 100% stock dividend and the par value per share remains at $20, the value of the capital stock would
   A. remain the same
   B. increase to $5,600,000
   C. increase to $5,000,000
   D. decrease

8. In a conventional form of the statement of sources and application of funds, which one of the following would NOT be included? — 8.____
   A. Periodic amortization of premium of bonds payable
   B. Machinery, fully depreciated and scrapped
   C. Patents written off
   D. Treasury stock purchased from a stockholder

Questions 9-11.

DIRECTIONS: Questions 9 through 11 are to be answered on the basis of the balance sheet shown below for the Argo, Baron and Schooster partnership.

Cash	$ 20,000
Other assets	180,000
Total	$200,000
Liabilities	$50,000
Argo Capital (40%)	37,000
Baron Capital (40%)	65,000
Schooster Capital (20%)	48,000
Total	$200,000

9. If George is to be admitted as a new 1/6 partner without recording goodwill or bonus, George should contribute cash of 9.____
   A. $40,000 B. $36,000 C. $33,333 D. $30,000

10. Assume that Schooster is paid $51,000 by George for his interest in the partnership. 10.____
    Which of the following choices shows the CORRECT revised capital account for each partner?
    A. Argo, $38,500; Baron, $66,500; George, $51,000
    B. Argo, $38,500; Baron, $66,500; George, $48,000
    C. Argo, $37,000; Baron, $65,000; George, $51,000
    D. Argo, $37,000; Baron, $65,000; George, $48,000

11. Assume that George had not been admitted as a partner but that the partnership was dissolved and liquidated on the basis of the original balance sheet. Non-cash assets with a book value of $90,000 were sold for $50,000 cash. After payment of creditors, all available cash was distributed. 11.____
    Which of the following choices MOST NEARLY shows what each of the partners would receive?
    A. Argo, $0; Baron, $13,333; Schooster, $6,667
    B. Argo, $0; Baron, $3,000; Schooster, $17,000
    C. Argo, $6,667; Baron, $6,667; Schooster, $6,666
    D. Argo, $8,000; Baron, $8,000; Schooster, $4,000

12. Which one of the following should be restricted to ONLY one employee in order to assure proper control of assets? 12.____
    A. Access to safe deposit box
    B. Placing orders and maintaining relationship with a principal vendor
    C. Collection of a particular past due account
    D. Custody of the petty cash fund

13. To assure proper internal control, the quantities of materials ordered may be omitted from that copy of the purchase order which is
    A. sent to the accounting department
    B. retained in the purchasing department
    C. sent to the party requisitioning the material
    D. sent to the receiving department

13.____

14. The Amey Corporation has an inventory of raw materials and parts made up of many different items which are of small value individually but of significant total value
    A BASIC control requirement in such a situation is that
    A. perpetual inventory records should be maintained for all items
    B. physical inventories should be taken on a cyclical basis rather than at year end
    C. storekeeping, production, and inventory record-keeping functions should be separated
    D. requisitions for materials should be approved by a corporate officer

14.____

15. In conducting an audit of plant assets, which of the following accounts MUST be examined in order to ascertain that additions to plant assets have been correctly stated and reflect charges that are properly capitalized?
    A. Accounts Receivable
    B. Sales Income
    C. Maintenance and Repairs
    D. Investments

15.____

16. Which one of the following is a control procedure that would prevent a vendor's invoice from being paid twice (once upon the original invoice and once upon the monthly statement?
    A. Attaching the receiving report to the disbursement support papers
    B. Prenumbering of disbursement vouchers
    C. Using a limit of reasonable test
    D. Prenumbering of receiving reports

16.____

17. A "cut-off" bank statement is received for the period December 1 to December 10, 2021. Very few of the checks listed on the November 30, 2021 bank reconciliation cleared during the cut-off period.
    Of the following, the MOST likely reason for this is
    A. kiting
    B. using certified checks rather than ordinary checks
    C. holding the cash disbursement book open after year end
    D. overstating year-end bank balance

17.____

18. "Lapping" is a common type of defalcation.
    Of the audit techniques listed below, the one MOST effective in the detection of "lapping" is
    A. reconciliation of year-end bank statements
    B. review of duplicate deposit slips
    C. securing confirmations from banks
    D. checking footings in cash journals

18.____

19. Of the following, the MOST common argument against the use of the negative accounts receivable confirmation is that 19.____
    A. cost per response is excessively high
    B. statistical sampling techniques cannot be applied to selection of the sample
    C. client's customers may assume that the confirmation is a request for payment
    D. lack of response does not necessarily indicate agreement with the balance

Questions 20-21.

DIRECTIONS Questions 20 and 21 are to be answered on the basis of the information in the Payroll Summary given below. This Payroll Summary represents payroll for a monthly period for a particular agency.

PAYROLL SUMMARY						
		Deductions				
Employee	Total Earnings	FICA	Withhold Tax	State Tax	Other	Net Pay
W	450.00	26.00	67.00	18.00	6.00	333.00
X	235.00	14.00	33.00	8.00	2.00	178.00
Y	341.00	20.00	52.00	14.00	5.00	250.00
Z	275.00	16.00	30.00	6.00	2.40	220.60
Totals	1,301.00	76.00	182.00	46.00	15.40	981.60

20. Based on the data given above, the amount of cash that would have to be available to pay the employees on payday is 20.____
    A. $1,301.00 B. $981.60 C. $905.60 D. $662.60

21. Based on the data given above, the amount of cash that would have to be governmental depository is 21.____
    A. $334.00 B. $182.00 C. $158.00 D. $76.00

Questions 22-23.

DIRECTIONS: Questions 22 and 23 are to be answered on the basis of the information given below concerning an imprest fund.

Assume a $1,020 imprest fund for cash expenditures is maintained in your agency. As an audit procedure, the fund is counted and the following information results from that count.

Unreimbursed bills properly authorized	$ 345.00
Check from employee T. Jones	125.00
Check from Supervisor R. Riggles	250.00
I.O.U. signed by employee J. Sloan	100.00
Cash counted–coins and bills	200.00
TOTAL	$1,020.00

22. A PROPER statement of cash on hand based upon the data shown above should show a balance of 22.____
    A. $1,020 B. $1,000 C. $545 D. $200

23. Based upon the data shown above, the account reflects IMPROPER handling of the fund because 23.____
    A. vouchers are unreimbursed
    B. the cash balance is too low
    C. employees have used it for loans and check-cashing purposes
    D. the unreimbursed bills should not have been authorized

Question 24-25.

DIRECTIONS: Questions 24 and 25 are to be answered on the basis of the following information.

The following information was taken from the ledgers of the Past Present Corporation:

Common stock had been issued for $6,000,000. This represents 400,000 shares of stock at a stated value of $5 per share. Fifty-thousand shares are in the treasury. These 50,000 shares were acquired for $25 per share. The total undistributed net income since the origin of the corporation was $3,750,000 as of December 31, 2021. Ten-thousand of the treasury stock shares were sold in January 2022 for $30 per share.

24. Based only on the information given above, the TOTAL stockholders' equity that should have been shown on the balance sheet as of December 31,2021 was 24.____
    A. $2,000,000 B. $6,000,000 C. $8,500,000 D. $9,750,000

25. Based only on the information given above, the Retained Earnings as of December 31, 2022 will be 25.____
    A. $2,000,000 B. $3,750,000 C. $3,800,000 D. $4,050,000

Questions 26-29.

DIRECTIONS: Questions 26 through 29 are to be answered on the basis of the following information.

A statement of income for the Dartmouth Corporation for the 2022 fiscal year follows:

Sales	$89,000	
Cost of Goods Sold	20,000	
Gross Margin		$34,000
Expenses		20,000
Net Income Before Income Taxes		$14,000
Provision for Income Taxes (50%)		7,000
Net Income		$7,000

The following errors were discovered relating to the 2022 fiscal year:

- Closing inventory was overstated by $2,100
- A $3,000 expenditure was capitalized during fiscal year 2022 that should have been listed under Expenses. This was subject to 10% amortization taken for a full year
- Sales included $3,500 of deposits received from customers for future orders.
- Accrued salaries of $850 were not included in Cost of Goods Sold
- Interest receivable of $500 was omitted

Assume that the books were not closed and that you have prepared a corrected income statement. Answer Questions 26 through 29 on the basis of your corrected income statement.

26. The gross margin after accounting for adjustments SHOULD BE 26.____
    A. $37,500 B. $35,400 C. $31,900 D. $27,550

27. The adjusted income before income taxes SHOULD BE 27.____
    A. $5,350 B. $9,550 C. $15,000 D. $15,850

28. The adjusted income after provision for a 50% tax rate SHOULD BE 28.____
    A. $7,925 B. $7,500 C. $4,500 D. $2,675

29. After making adjustments, sales to be reported for fiscal year 2022 SHOULD BE 29.____
    A. unchanged B. increased by $3,500
    C. decreased by $3,500 D. reduced by $2,100

Questions 30-33.

DIRECTIONS: Questions 30 through 33 are to be answered on the basis of the following budget for the Utility Corporation for 2022.

Sales	$550,000
Cost of Goods Sold	320,000
Selling Expenses	75,000
General Expenses	60,000
Net Income	95,000

30. If sales are actually 12% above the budget, then ACTUAL sales will be 30.____
    A. $550,000 B. $562,000 C. $605,000 D. $616,000

31. If actual costs of goods sold exceed the budget by 10%, then the cost of goods sold will be 31.____
    A. $294,400 B. $320,000 C. $605,000 D. $352,000

32. If selling expenses exceed the budget by 10%, the INCREASE in the selling expenses will be 32.____
    A. $750 B. $3,750 C. $7,500 D. $8,333

33. If general expenses are under budget by 5%, they will amount to 33.____
A. $3,000 B. $57,000 C. $60,000 D. $63,000

Questions 34-35.

DIRECTIONS: Questions 34 and 35 are to be answered on the basis of the following information.

The Yontiff Company began business on January 2, 2021. During the first month, credit sales totaled $100,000. During February, credit sales totaled $125,000. 70% of credit sales are paid during the month of sale, and the balance is collected during the following month.

34. During the month of January, cash collections on credit sales totaled 34.____
A. $70,000 B. $95,000 C. $100,000 D. $125,000

35. During the month of February, cash collections on credit sales totaled 35.____
A. $70,000 B. $87,500 C. $117,505 D. $125,000

Questions 36-38.

DIRECTIONS: Questions 36 through 38 are to be answered on the basis of the following information taken from the balance sheet of the F Corporation.

Common Stock $200 Par	$1,400,000
Premium on Common Stock	115,000
Deficit	50,000

36. The number of shares of common stock outstanding is 36.____
A. 200 B. 700 C. 7,000 D. 14,000

37. The total equity is 37.____
A. $50,000 B. $115,000 C. $1,400,000 D. $1,465,000

38. The book value per share of stock is MOST NEARLY 38.____
A. $160 B. $200 C. $209 D. $312

Questions 39-40.

DIRECTIONS: Questions 39 and 40 are to be answered on the basis of the following statement.

You are examining the expense accounts of a contractor and you discover that, although his payroll records show proper deductions from employees, he has never provided for the payroll tax expenses for these employees.

39. As a result of the oversight described in the above statement, the Costs of Construction in Progress as given on the balance sheet will be _____ on the balance sheet. 39.____
A. understated B. overstated C. unaffected D. omitted

40. As a result of the oversight described in the above statement, the balance sheet for the firm will reflect an 40.____
A. overstatement of liabilities
B. understatement of liabilities
C. overstatement of assets
D. understatement of assets

KEY (CORRECT ANSWERS)

1.	B	11.	D	21.	A	31.	D
2.	C	12.	D	22.	D	32.	C
3.	A	13.	D	23.	C	33.	B
4.	C	14.	C	24.	C	34.	A
5.	B	15.	C	25.	B	35.	C
6.	A	16.	A	26.	D	36.	C
7.	A	17.	C	27.	A	37.	D
8.	B	18.	B	28.	D	38.	C
9.	D	19.	D	29.	C	39.	A
10.	D	20.	B	30.	D	40.	B

TEST 2

DIRECTIONS: Each question or incomplete statement is followed by several suggested answers or completions. Select the one that BEST answers the question or completes the statement. *PRINT THE LETTER OF THE CORRECT ANSWER IN THE SPACE AT THE RIGHT.*

Questions 1-4.

DIRECTIONS: Questions 1 through 4 are to be answered on the basis of the following information.

In the audit of the Audell Co. for the calendar year 2021, the accountant noted the following errors.

- An adjusting entry for $10 for interest accrued on a customer's $4,000, 60-day, 6% note was not recorded at the end of December 2020. In 2021, the total interest received was credited to interest income.
- Equipment was leased on December 31, 2020 and rental of $300 was paid in advance for the next three months and charged to Rent Expense.
- On November 1, 2020, space was rented at $75 per month. The tenant paid six months rent in advance which was credited to Rent Income.
- Salary expenses in the amount of $60 were not recorded at the end of 2020
- Depreciation in the amount of $80 was not recorded at the end of 2020.
- An error of $200 in addition on the year-end 2020 physical inventory sheets was made. The inventory was overstated.

1. The amount of the net adjustment to Net Income for 2020 is 1.____
   A. Credit $430 B. Debit $430 C. Credit $600 D. Credit $560

2. The net change in asset values at December 31, 2020 is 2.____
   A. Credit $70 B. Debit $70 C. Debit $110 D. Credit $60

3. The net change in liabilities at December 31, 2020 is 3.____
   A. Debit $360 B. Credit $430 C. Debit $560 D. Credit $360

4. The net change in Owner's Equity at December 31, 2020 is 4.____
   A. Debit $720 B. Debit $430 C. Credit $320 D. Credit $720

5. As of October 2, 2021, the Mallory Company's books reflect a balance of $2,104.75 in its account entitled Cash in Bank. A comparison of the book entries with the bank statement showed the following: 5.____
   - A check in the amount of $76.25 outstanding at the end of September 2021 had not been returned.
   - One check, which was returned with the October bank statement, in the amount of $247 had been recorded in the October c ash book as $274.
   - A total of $139 of checks issued in October had not been returned with the October bank statement.
   - A deposit of $65 was returned by the bank because of insufficient funds.

- The bank charged a service charge of $3.25 for the month of October which as not reported on the books until November.
- The bank had credited $247 representing a note collected in the amount of $250 which was not picked up on the books until November.
- A deposit of $305.50 was recorded on the books in October but not on the bank statement.

The balance in the bank as shown on the bank statement at October 31, 2021 is
A. $2,220.25 B. $2,104.75 C. $2,006.25 D. $2,315.25

Questions 6-8.

DIRECTIONS: Questions 6 through 8 are to be answered on the basis of the following information.

A company purchased three cars at $3,150 each on April 2, 2021. Depreciation is to be computed on a mileage basis. The estimated mileage to be considered is 50,000 miles, with a trade-in value of $650 for each car.

After having been driven 8,400 miles, car #1 was completely destroyed on November 23, 2020 and not replaced. The insurance company paid $2,500 for the loss.

As of December 31, 2020, of the two remaining cars, car #2 had been driven 10,300 miles and car #3 was driven 11,500 miles.

On July 10, 2021, after having been driven a total of 24,600 miles, car #2 was sold for $1,800.

Car #3, after having been driven a total of 27,800 miles, was traded in on December 28, 2021 for a new car (#4) that had a list price of $3,000. On the purchase of car #4, the dealer allowed a trade-in value of $1,850.

6. The balance in the Allowance for Depreciation account at December 31, 2020 is 6.____
A. $1,850 B. $910 C. $1,090 D. $1,110

7. The depreciation expense for the calendar year 2021 is 7.____
A. $1,530 B. $2,000 C. $2,500 D. $3,00

8. The book value of the new car (car #4) using the income tax method is 8.____
A. $1,850 B. $3,000 C. $2,500 D. $2,910

Questions 9-10.

DIRECTIONS: Questions 9 and 10 are to be answered on the basis of the following information.

The Pneumatic Corp. showed the following balance sheets at December 31, 2020 and December 31, 2021

	12/31/2020	12/31/2021
Cash	$6,700	$9,000
Accounts Receivable	12,000	11,500
Merchandise Inventory	31,500	32,000
Prepaid Expenses	800	1,000
Equipment	21,000	28,000
	$72,000	$81,500
Accumulated Depreciation	$4,000	$5,500
Accounts Payable	17,500	11,500
Common Stock - $5 Per Share	10,000	5,000
Premium on Common Stock	40,000	50,000
Retained Earnings	10,500	13,000
	$72,000	$81,500

Additional Information:
A further examination of the Pneumatic Corp.'s transactions for 2021 showed the following:

- Depreciation on equipment, $2,500]
- Fully depreciated equipment that cost $1,000 was scrapped, and cost and related accumulated depreciation eliminated.
- Two thousand shares of common stock were sold at $6 per share.
- A cash dividend of $10,000 was paid.

9. A statement of funds provided and applied for the calendar year 2021 would show that net income provided funds in the amount of 9.____
   A. $2,500 B. $9,500 C. $15,000 D. $22,500

10. The funds applied to the acquisition of equipment during the calendar year 2021 amounts to 10.____
    A. $21,000 B. $28,000 C. $1,000 D. $8,000

11. A company's Wage Expense account had a $19,100 debit balance before any adjustment at the end of its December 31, 2020 fiscal year. The company employs five individuals who earn $15 per day and were paid on Friday for the five days ending on Friday, December 25, 2020. All employees worked during the week ending January 2, 2021. 11.____
    The adjusted balance in the Wage Expense account at December 31, 2020 is
    A. $22,300 B. $19,100 C. $19,250 D. $19,325

Questions 12-13.

DIRECTIONS: Questions 12 and 13 are to be answered on the basis of the following information.

The Peach Corp.'s books reflect an account entitled "Allowance for Bad Debts" showing a credit balance of $1,510 as of January 1, 2020.

During 2020, it wrote off 735 of bad debts and increased the allowance for bad debts by an amount equal to ¼ of 1% of sales of $408,000.

During 2021, it wrote off $605 as bad debts and recorded $50 of a debt that had been previously written off.

An addition to the "Allowance for Bad Debts" was provided based upon ¼ of 1% on $478,000 of sales.

12. The balance in the "Allowance for Bad Debts" account at December 31, 2021 is 12.____
    A. $2,550 B. $2,434 C. $2,360 D. $2,240

13. The amount of the Bad Debt expense for the calendar year 2021 is 13.____
    A. $1,195 B. $1,405 C. $2,000 D. $1,510

14. The following ratio is based upon the 2021 financial statements of the Chino Corp.: 14.____
    Number of Times Bond Interest Earned: $28,000/$3,000 = 9.33 times
    Information relating to the corrections of the income data for 2021 follows:
    - Rental payment for December 2021 at $2,00 per month had been recorded in January 2022. No provision has been made for this expense on the 2021 books.
    - During 2021, merchandise shipped on consignment and unsold had been recorded as

Debit – Accounts Receivable	$4,000
Credit – Sales	4,000

    (Note: The inventory of this merchandise was properly recorded.)
    If the described ratio, Number of Times Bond Interest Earned, was recomputed, taking into consideration the corrections listed above and ignoring tax factors in the calculations, the recomputed Number of Times Bond Interest Earned would be _____ times.
    A. 8.10 B. 7.60 C. 6.20 D. 5.10

Questions 15-16.

DIRECTIONS: Questions 15 and 16 are to be answered on the basis of the following information.

The Delancey Department Store, Inc. sells merchandise on the installment basis. The selling price of its merchandise is $500 and its cost is $325.

At the end of its fiscal year, an examination of its accounts showed the following:

Sales (Installment	$500,000
Installment Accounts Receivable	280,000
Sales Commissions	15,000
Other Expenses	32,000

15. The net income for the fiscal year, before taxes, using the installment method of reporting income, is 15.____
A. $30,000 B. $20,000 C. $15,000 D. $35,000

16. The balance in the Deferred Income Account at the end of the fiscal year is 16.____
A. $110,000 B. $80,000 C. $76,000 D. $98,000

Questions 17-18.

DIRECTIONS: Questions 17 and 18 are to be answered on the basis of the following information.

The Merrimac Company sold 8,800 units of a product at $5 per unit during the calendar year 2021. In addition, it has the following transactions:

	Units	Unit Cost
Inventory – January 1, 2021	1,000	$2.80
Purchases – March	1,000	3.00
June	4,000	3.20
September	3,000	3.30
October	1,000	3.50

17. If we assume that selling and administrative expenses cost $8,800, the Net Income for the calendar year 2021, using the first-in first-out method of costing inventory is 17.____
A. $8,460 B. $7,360 C. $6,600 D. $4,070

18. If we assume that selling and administrative expenses cost $8,800, the Net Income for the calendar year 2021, using the last-in first-out method of costing inventory, is 18.____
A. $4,550 B. $7,360 C. $6,600 D. $5,000

19. L. Eron and A. Pilott are partners who share income and losses in the ratio 3:2, respectively. The balance in the Profit and Loss account on December 31, 2021, prior to distribution to the partners, is $20,800. Before distributing any profits to the partnership in the agreed ratio, L. Eron is to be given credit for interest on his loan of $60,000, outstanding for the entire year, at 6% per annum. A. Pilott is to receive a bonus of 10% of the net income over $5,100, after deducting the bonus to himself and the interest to L. Eron. 19.____
Giving consideration to all the above information, the total amount of net income to be credited to A. Pilott is
A. $8,320 B. $2,080 C. $7,540 D. $15,700

Questions 20-21.

DIRECTIONS: Questions 20 and 21 are to be answered on the basis of the following information.

Schneider and Samuels are partners with capital balances on December 31, 2021 of $15,000 and $25,000, respectively. They share profits in a ratio of 2:1.

Goroff is to be admitted to the partnership. He agrees to be admitted as a partner with a cash investment to give him a one-third interest in the capital and profits of the business. All the parties agree that the goodwill to be granted to Goroff should be valued at $6,000.

20. The required cash to cover Goroff's investment in a business partnership according to the terms stated is 20.____
    A. $20,000 B. $14,000 C. $6,000 D. $25,000

21. After his cash investment, and all other initial entries, the credit to Goroff's Capital account is 21.____
    A. $20,000 B. $14,000 C. $6,000 D. $25,000

22. The Marlin Corp. sold 7,800 units of its product at $25 per unit and suffered a net loss for its calendar year ending December 31, 2021 of $2,000. The fixed expenses amounted to $80,000 and the variable expenses $117,000. The Marlin Corp. believes that by expending $20,000 in an advertising campaign, it could increase its sales, retaining the $25 per unit selling price, to generate a profit. 22.____
    Assuming the above facts, the sales revenue for 2021 reflecting the break-even point is
    A. $195,000 B. $217,000 C. $250,000 D. $300,000

23. The Anide Corp., which keeps its books on the accrual basis, had the following transactions for its calendar year ending December 31, 2021. 23.____
    - April 15, 2021 – Authorized the issuance of $3,000,000 of 5.5%, 20 year bonds, dated May 1, 2021. Interest to be paid November 1 and May 1.
    - June 1, 2021 – Sold the entire issue at $2,965,150 plus accrued interest
    - November 1, 2021 – Paid the interest due.

    The interest expense for the calendar year 2021 is
    A. $85,000 B. $165,000 C. $110,000 D. $97,300

Questions 24-26.

DIRECTIONS: Questions 24 through 26 are to be answered on the basis of the following information.

The following information was taken from a worksheet that was used in the preparation of the balance sheet and the profit and loss statement of the Hott Company for 2021.

The Balance Sheet Contained	Amount
Travel Expense Unpaid	$995
Legal and Collection Fees – Prepaid in Advance	672
Interest Received in Advance	469

The Profit and Loss Statement Contained	Amount
Travel Expenses	$7,343
Legal and Collection Fees	5,461
Interest Income	3,114

The proper adjusting and closing entries were made on the books of the company by the accountant and the described information was reported on the financial statements. The books are kept on an accrual basis.

On the basis of the above facts, the balance in each of the following accounts in the trial balance, before adjusting and closing entries were made, was as follows:

24. Travel Expense Account 24.____
A. $8,338 B. $7,343 C. $6,348 D. $995

25. Legal and Collection Fees Account 25.____
A. $672 B. $4,789 C. $5,461 D. $6,133

26. Interest Income Account 26.____
A. $3,583 B. $3,114 C. $2,645 D. $469

Questions 27-28.

DIRECTIONS: Questions 27 and 28 are to be answered on the basis of the following information

The following is the stockholder's equity section of a corporation:

Preferred Stock (7%, cumulative, non-participating, $100 par value , 5,000 shares issued and outstanding)	$500.000
Common Stock ($1.00 par value, 500,000, issued and outstanding)	500,000
	$1,000,000
Deficit	(40,000)
	$960,000

27. Assuming two years' dividends in arrears on the preferred stock, the book value per share of common stock is 27.____
A. 78¢ B. 80¢ C. 63¢ D. 94¢

28. Assuming two years' dividends in arrears on the preferred stock, the book value per share of preferred stock is 28.____
A. $130 B. $114 C. $98 D. $140

Questions 29-30.

DIRECTIONS: Questions 29 and 30 are to be answered on the basis of the following information.

Regina Corporation on December 31, 2021 had the following stockholder's equity:

Common Stock ($10 par value), 10,000 shares authorized and outstanding)	$100,000
Retained Earnings	20,000
	$120,000

On December 31, 2021, the Astro Corp. purchased 9,000 shares of the Regina Corporation's outstanding shares, paying $14 per share

29. The entry to eliminate Astro Corp.'s investment and the Regina Corporation's stockholder's equity on consolidation would show a debit or credit to an account called "Excess of Cost Over Book Value" of 29.____
    A. Credit, $18,000
    B. Debit, $18,000
    C. Debit, $15,000
    D. Debit, $19,000

30. If the Regina Corporation had earnings for the calendar year 2021 of $10,000 and had paid out $8,000 of these earnings as dividends, and an entry to eliminate the Astro Corp.'s investment and the Regina Corporation's stockholder's equity were made, the minority stockholder's equity would be 30.____
    A. $15,000
    B. $10,100
    C. $12,200
    D. $14,800

KEY (CORRECT ANSWERS)

1.	B	11.	D	21.	A
2.	A	12.	B	22.	C
3.	D	13.	A	23.	D
4.	B	14.	B	24.	C
5.	A	15.	A	25.	D
6.	C	16.	D	26.	A
7.	A	17.	B	27.	A
8.	D	18.	C	28.	B
9.	C	19.	C	29.	B
10.	D	20.	B	30.	C

TEST 3

DIRECTIONS: Each question or incomplete statement is followed by several suggested answers or completions. Select the one that BEST answers the question or completes the statement. *PRINT THE LETTER OF THE CORRECT ANSWER IN THE SPACE AT THE RIGHT.*

1. For the measurement of net income to be as realistic as possible, it is DESIRABLE that revenue be recognized at the point that 1.____
   A. cash is collected from customers
   B. an order for merchandise or services is received from a customer
   C. a deposit or advance payment is received from a customer
   D. goods are delivered or services are rendered to customers

2. An accounting principle must receive substantial authoritative support to qualify as "generally accepted." 2.____
   Many organizations and agencies have been influential in the development of generally accepted accounting principles, but the MOST influential leadership has come from the
   A. New York Stock Exchange
   B. American Institute of Certified Public Accountants
   C. Securities and Exchange Commission
   D. American Accounting Association

3. In which one of the following ways does the declaration and payment of a cash dividend affect corporate net income? It ______ net income. 3.____
   A. does not affect
   B. reduces
   C. increases
   D. capitalizes

4. Under which one of the following headings of the corporate balance sheet should the liability for a dividend payable in stock appear? 4.____
   A. Current Liabilities
   B. Long Term Liabilities
   C. Stockholders' Equity
   D. Current Assets

5. In which one of the following is "Working Capital" MOST likely to be found? 5.____
   A. Income Statement
   B. Analysis of Retained Earnings
   C. Computation of Cost of Capital
   D. Statement of Funds Provided and Applied

6. Which one of the following procedures is NOT generally mandatory in auditing a merchandising corporation? 6.____
   A. Physical observation of inventory count
   B. Written circularization of accounts receivable
   C. Confirmation of bank balance
   D. Circularization of the stockholders

7. A company purchased office supplies during 2021 in the total amount of $1,400 and charged the entire amount to the asset account. An inventory of supplies taken on December 31, 2021 shows the cost of unused supplies to be $250. The entry to record this fact, assuming the books have not been closed, involves

A. credit to capital
B. debit to supplies Expense
C. credit to supplies expense
D. debit to supplies on hand

7.____

8. A corporation's records show $600,000 (credit) in net sales, $200,000 (debit) in year-end accounts receivable, and $2,000 (debit) in Allowance for Bad Debts. The company's aged schedule of accounts receivable indicates a probable future loss from failure to collect year-end receivables in the amount of $6,000.
Of the following, the MOST correct entry to adjust the Allowance for Bad Debts at year-end is

A. $1,000 credit
B. $4,000 credit
C. $8,000 debit
D. $8,000 credit

8.____

Questions 9-10.

DIRECTIONS: Questions 9 and 10 are to be answered on the basis of the following information.

A company commenced business in 2021 and purchased inventory as follows:

March	100 units @	$5	$500
June	300	6	1,800
October	200	7	1,400
November	500	6	3,500
December	100	6	600
TOTAL	1,200		$7,800

**Units sold in 2021 amounted to 1,200

9. Under the LIFO inventory principle, the value of the remaining inventory is

A. $1,700
B. $1,875
C. $2,145
D. $2,225

9.____

10. Under the FIFO inventory principle, the value of the remaining inventory is

A. $1,650
B. $1,875
C. $2,000
D. $2,025

10.____

11. When doing a trial balance, assume that, as a result of a single error, the total of the credit balances is greater than the total of the debit balances. Which one of the following single errors could NOT be the cause of this discrepancy?

A. Failure to post a debit
B. Posting a debit as a credit
C. Failure to post a credit
D. Posting a credit twice

11.____

Questions 12-13.

DIRECTIONS: Questions 12 and 13 are to be answered on the basis of the following information.

A and B are partners with capital balances of $20,000 and $30,000, respectively, at June 30, 2021, who share profits and losses, 40% and 60%, respectively. On July 1, 2021, C is to be admitted into the partnership under the following conditions:

- Partnership assets are to be revalued and increased by $10,000
- C is to invest $40,000 but be credited for $30,000 while the remaining $10,000 is to be credited to A and B to compensate them for their pre-existing goodwill.

12. After C is admitted and the proper entries are made, A's capital account will have a credit balance of 12.____
    A. $24,500 B. $28,000 C. $30,200 D. $36,000

13. After the admission of C to the partnership, C's share of profits and losses is agreed upon at 20%. 13.____
    Assuming no other adjustments, the new percentage for profit and loss distribution to A will be
    A. 18% B. 32% C. 36% D. 45%

14. A company reports as income for tax purposes $70,000 and its book income before the provision for income taxes is $100,000. 14.____
    Assuming a 50% tax rate, the PROPER tax expense to be recorded following tax allocation procedures is
    A. $33,000 B. $40,000 C. $50,000 D. $60,000

15. The relationship between the total of cash and current receivables to total current liabilities is commonly referred to by accountants as the 15.____
    A. acid-test ratio
    B. cross-statement ratio
    C. current ratio
    D. R.O.I. ratio

16. On a statement of sources and application of funds, the depreciation expense is normally shown as a(n) 16.____
    A. addition to operating income
    B. subtraction from funds provided
    C. addition to funds applied
    D. reduction from operating income

17. Company A owns 100% of the capital stock of Company B and reports on a consolidated basis. During the year, Company A sold inventory to Company B at a profit of $100,000. One-half of this inventory has been sold at year-end by Company B to the public. 17.____
    Which one of the following would be the MOST correct adjustment, if any, to make the consolidated retained earnings conform to generally accepted accounting principles?
    A. Decrease by $50,000
    B. Increase by $50,000
    C. Increase by $100,000
    D. No adjustment

18. X, Y, and Z are partners with capital of $11,000, $12,000, and $4,500. X has a loan due from the partnership to him of $2,000. Profits and losses are shared in the ratio of 4:5:1, respectively. The partnership has paid off all outside liabilities, and its remaining assets consist of $9,000 in cash and $20,500 of accounts receivable. The partners agree to disburse the $9,000 to themselves in such a way that, even if one of the receivables is realized, no partner will have been overpaid.
Under these conditions, which of the following MOST NEARLY represents the amount to be paid to partner X?
A. $1,960 B. $3,200 C. $4,800 D. $5,000

18.____

19. R Company needs $2,000,000 to finance an expansion of plant facilities. The company expects to earn a return of 15% on this investment before considering the cost of capital or income taxes. The average income tax rate for the R Company is 40%.
If the company raises the funds by issuing 6% bonds at face value, the earnings available to common stockholders after the new plant facilities are in operation may be expected to increase by
A. $65,000 B. $70,000 C. $108,000 D. $116,000

19.____

20. The budget for a given factory overhead cost was $150,000 for the year. The actual cost for the year was $125,000.
Based on these facts, it can be said that the plant manager has done a better job than expected in controlling this cost if the cost is a
A. semi-variable cost
B. variable cost and actual production was 83 1/3% of budgeted production
C. semi-variable cost which includes a fixed element of $25,000 per period
D. variable cost and actual production was equal to budgeted production

20.____

21. The Home Office account on the books of the City Branch shows a credit balance of $15,000 at the end of a year and the City Branch account on the books of the Home Office shows a debit balance of $12,000.
Of the following, the MOST likely reason for the discrepancy in the two accounts is that
A. merchandise shipped by the Home Office to the branch has not been recorded by the branch
B. the Home Office has not recorded a branch loss for the first quarter of the year
C. the branch has just mailed a check for $3,000 to the Home Office which has not yet been received by the Home Office
D. the Home Office has not yet recorded the branch profit for the first quarter of the year

21.____

22. The concept of matching costs and revenues means that
A. the expenses offset against revenues should be related to the same time period
B. revenues are at least as great as expenses on the average
C. revenues and expenses are equal
D. net income equals revenues minus expenses for the same earning period

22.____

23. If the inventory at the end of the current year is understated, and the error is not caught during the following year, the effect is to 23.____
    A. *overstate* the income for the two-year period
    B. *overstate* income this year and *understate* income next year
    C. *understate* income this year and *overstate* income next year
    D. *understate* income this year, with no effect on the income of the next year

---

KEY (CORRECT ANSWERS)

1. D
2. B
3. A
4. C
5. D

6. D
7. B
8. D
9. A
10. C

11. C
12. B
13. B
14. C
15. A

16. A
17. A
18. C
19. C
20. D

21. D
22. A
23. C

EXAMINATION SECTION

TEST 1

DIRECTIONS: Each question or incomplete statement is followed by several suggested answers or completions. Select the one that BEST answers the question or completes the statement. *PRINT THE LETTER OF THE CORRECT ANSWER IN THE SPACE AT THE RIGHT.*

1. Gross income of an individual for Federal income tax purposes does NOT include — 1.____
   A. interest credited to a bank savings account
   B. gain from the sale of sewer authority bonds
   C. back pay received as a result of job reinstatement
   D. interest received from State Dormitory Authority bonds

2. A cash-basis, calendar-year taxpayer purchased an annuity policy at a total cost of $20,000. Starting on January 1 of 2022, he began to receive annual payments of $1,500. His life expectancy as of that date was 16 years. The amount of annuity income to be included in his gross income for the taxable year 2022 is — 2.____
   A. none B. $250 C. $1,250 D. $1,500

3. The transactions related to a municipal police retirement system should be included in a(n) _____ fund. — 3.____
   A. intra-governmental service B. trust
   C. general D. special revenue

4. The budget for a given cost during a given period was $100,000. The actual cost for the period was $90,000. Based upon these facts, one should say that the responsible manager has done a better than expected job in controlling the cost if the cost is _____ budgeted production. — 4.____
   A. variable and actual production equaled
   B. a discretionary fixed cost and actual production equaled
   C. variable and actual production was 90% of
   D. variable and actual production was 80% of

5. In the conduct of an audit, the MOST practical method by which an accountant can satisfy himself as to the physical existence of inventory is to — 5.____
   A. be present and observe personally the audited firm's physical inventory being taken
   B. independently verify an adequate proportion of all inventory operations performed by the audited firm
   C. mail confirmation requests to vendors of merchandise sold to the audited firm within the inventory year
   D. review beforehand the adequacy of the audited firm's plan for inventory taking, and during the actual inventory-taking states, verify that this plan is being followed

Questions 6-7.

DIRECTIONS: Questions 6 and 7 are to be answered on the basis of the following information.

For the month of March, the ABC Manufacturing Corporation's estimated factory overhead for an expected volume of 15,000 lbs. of a product was as follows:

	Amount	Overhead Rate Per Unit
Fixed Overhead	$3,000	$.20
Variable Overhead	$9,000	$.60

Actual volume was 10,000 lbs. and actual overhead expense was $7,700.

6. The Spending (Budget) Variance was _____ (Favorable). 6._____
   A. $1,300 B. $6,000 C. $7,700 D. $9,000

7. The Idle Capacity Variance was 7._____
   A. $300 (Favorable) B. $1,000 (Unfavorable)
   C. $1,300 (Favorable) D. $8,000 (Unfavorable)

Questions 8-11.

DIRECTIONS: Questions 8 through 11 are to be answered on the basis of the following information.

A bookkeeper, who was not familiar with proper accounting procedures, prepared the following financial report for Largor Corporation as of December 31, 2021. In addition to the errors in presentation, additional data below was not considered in the preparation of the report. Restate this balance sheet in proper form, giving recognition to the additional data, so that you will be able to determine the required information to answer Questions 8 through 11.

LARGOR CORPORATION
December 31, 2021

Current Assets			
Cash		$110,000	
Marketable Securities		53,000	
Accounts Receivable	$261,400		
Accounts Payable	125,000	136,400	
Inventories		274,000	
Prepaid Expenses		24,000	
Treasury Stock		20,000	
Cash Surrender Value of Officers' Life Insurance Policies		105,000	$722,400
Plant Assets			
Equipment		350,000	
Building	200,000		
Reserve for Plant Expansion	75,000	125,000	
Land		47,500	
TOTAL ASSETS			$1,244,900

Liabilities			
Salaries Payable		16,500	
Cash Dividend Payable		50,000	
Stock Dividend Payable		70,000	
Bonds Payable	200,000		
Less Sinking Fund	90,000	110,000	
TOTAL LIABILITIES			$246,500
Stockholders' Equity:			
Paid In Capital			
Common Stock		350,000	
Retained Earnings and Reserves			
Reserve for Income Taxes	90,000		
Reserve for Doubtful Accounts	6,500		
Reserve for Treasury Stock	20,000		
Reserve for Depreciation Equipment	70,000		
Reserve for Depreciation Building	80,000		
Premium on Common Stock	15,000		
Retained Earnings	366,900	648,400	998,400
TOTAL LIABILITIES & EQUITY			1,244,900

Additional Data

A. Bond Payable will mature eight (8) years from Balance Sheet date.
B. The Stock Dividend Payable was declared on December 31, 2021.
C. The Reserve for Income Taxes represents the balance due on the estimated liability for taxes on income for the year ended December 31.
D. Advances from Customers at the Balance Sheet date totaled $13,600. This total is still credited against Accounts Receivable.
E. Prepaid Expenses include Unamortized Mortgage Costs of $15,000.
F. Marketable Securities were recorded at cost. Their market value at December 31, 2021 was $50,800.

8. After restatement of the balance sheet in proper form and giving recognition to the additional data, the Total Current Assets should be 8.____
   A. $597,400 B. $702,400 C. $712,300 D. $827,300

9. After restatement of the balance sheet in proper form and giving recognition to the additional data, the Total Current Liabilities should be 9.____
   A. $261,500 B. $281,500 C. $295,100 D. $370,100

10. After restatement of the balance sheet in proper form and giving recognition to the additional data, the net book value of plant and equipment should be 10.____
   A. $400,000 B. $447,500 C. $550,000 D. $597,500

11. After restatement of the balance sheet in proper form and giving recognition to the additional data, the Stockholders Equity should be 11.____
   A. $320,000 B. $335,000 C. $764,700 D. $874,700

12. When preparing the financial statement, dividends in arrears on preferred stock should be treated as a 12.____
    A. contingent liability
    B. deduction from capital
    C. parenthetical remark
    D. valuation reserve

13. The IPC Corporation has an intangible asset which it values at $1,000,000 and has a life expectancy of 60 years. 13.____
    The appropriate span of write-off, as determined by good accounting practice, should be _____ years.
    A. 17
    B. 34
    C. 40
    D. 60

14. The following information was used in costing inventory on October 31: 14.____

October				
	1 -	Beginning inventory	800 units	@ $1.20
	4 -	Received	200 units	@ $1.40
	16 -	Issued	400 units	
	24 -	Received	200 units	@ $1.60
	27 -	Issued	500 units	

    Using the LIFO method of inventory evaluation (end-of-month method), the total dollar value of the inventory at October 31 was
    A. $360
    B. $460
    C. $600
    D. $1,200

15. If a $400,000 par value bond issue paying 8%, with interest dates of June 30 and December 31, is sold in November 1 for par plus accrued interest, the cash proceeds received by the issuer on November 1 should be APPROXIMATELY 15.____
    A. $405,000
    B. $408,000
    C. $411,000
    D. $416,000

16. The TOTAL interest cost to the issuer of a bond issue sold for more than its face value is the periodic interest payment _____ amortization. 16.____
    A. plus the discount
    B. plus the premium
    C. minus the discount
    D. minus the premium

17. If shareholders donate shares of stock back to the company, such stock received by the company is properly classified as 17.____
    A. Treasury stock
    B. Unissued stock
    C. Other assets – investment
    D. Current assets - investment

18. Assume the following transactions have occurred: 18.____
    1. 10,000 shares of capital stock of Omer Corp., par value $50, have been sold and issued on initial sale @ $55 per share during the month of June
    2. 2,000 shares of previously issued stock were purchased from shareholders during the month of September @ $58 per share.

    As of September 30, the stockholders' equity section TOTAL should be
    A. $434,000
    B. $450,000
    C. $480,000
    D. $550,000

19. Mr. Diak, a calendar-year taxpayer in the construction business, agrees to construct a building for the Supermat Corporation to cost a total of $500,000 and to require about two years to complete. By December 31, 2021, he has expended $150,000 in costs, and it was determined that the building was 35% completed.
If Mr. Diak is reporting income under the completed contract method, the amount of gross income he will report for 2021 is
A. none B. $25,000 C. $175,000 D. $350,000

19.____

20. When the Board of Directors of a firm uses the present-value technique to aid in deciding whether or not to buy a new plant asset, it needs to have information reflecting
A. the cost of the new asset only
B. the increased production from use of new asset only
C. an estimated rate of return
D. the book value of the asset

20.____

KEY (CORRECT ANSWERS)

1.	D	11.	D
2.	B	12.	C
3.	B	13.	C
4.	A	14.	A
5.	D	15.	C
6.	A	16.	D
7.	B	17.	A
8.	C	18.	A
9.	C	19.	A
10.	B	20.	C

TEST 2

DIRECTIONS: Each question or incomplete statement is followed by several suggested answers or completions. Select the one that BEST answers the question or completes the statement. *PRINT THE LETTER OF THE CORRECT ANSWER IN THE SPACE AT THE RIGHT.*

Questions 1-3.

DIRECTIONS: Questions 1 through 3 are to be answered on the basis of the following information.

During your audit of the Avon Company, you find the following errors in the records of the company:

1. Incorrect exclusion from the final inventory of items costing $3,000 for which the purchase was not recorded.
2. Inclusion in the final inventory of goods costing $5,000, although a purchase was not recorded. The goods in question were being held on consignment from Reldrey Company.
3. Incorrect exclusion of $2,000 from the inventory count at the end of the period. The goods were in transit (F.O.B. shipping point); the invoice had been received and the purchase recorded.
4. Inclusion of items on the receiving dock that were being held for return to the vendor because of damage. In counting the goods in the receiving department, these items were incorrectly included. With respect to these goods, a purchase of $4,000 had been recorded.

The records (uncorrected) showed the following amounts:

1. Purchases, $170,000
2. Pretax income, $15,000
3. Accounts payable, $20,000; and
4. Inventory at the end of the period, $40,000.

1. The CORRECTED inventory is 1.____
   A. $36,000 B. $42,000 C. $43,000 D. $44,000

2. The CORRECTED income for the year is 2.____
   A. $12,000 B. $15,000 C. $17,000 D. $18,000

3. The CORRECT accounts payable liabilities are 3.____
   A. $16,000 B. $17,000 C. $19,000 D. $23,000

4. An auditing procedure that is MOST likely to reveal the existence of a contingent liability is 4.____
   A. a review of vouchers paid during the month following the year end
   B. confirmation of accounts payable
   C. an inquiry directed to legal counsel
   D. confirmation of mortgage notes

Questions 5-6.

DIRECTIONS: Questions 5 and 6 are to be answered on the basis of the following information.

Mr. Zelev operates a business as a sole proprietor and uses the cash basis for reporting income for income tax purposes. His bank account during 2021 for the business shows receipts totaling $285,000 and cash payments totaling $240,000. Included in the cash payments were payments for three-year business insurance policies whose premiums totaled $1,575. It was determined that the expired premiums for this year were $475. Further examination of the accounts and discussion with Mr. Zelev revealed the fact that included in the receipts were the following items, as well as the proceeds received from customers:

$15,000 which Mr. Zelev took from his savings account and deposited in the business account.

$20,000 which Mr. Zelev received from the bank as a loan which will be repaid next year.

Included in the cash payments were $10,000, which Mr. Zelev took on a weekly basis from the business receipts to use for his personal expenses.

5. The amount of net income to be reported for income tax purposes for calendar year 2022 for Mr. Zelev is 5.____
   A. $21,100 B. $26,100 C. $31,100 D. $46,100

6. Assuming the same facts as those reported above, Mr. Zelev would be required to pay a self-employment tax for 2022 of 6.____
   $895.05 B. $1,208.70 C. $1,234.35 D. $1,666.90

7. For the year ended December 2021, you are given the following information relative to the income and expense statements for the Sungam Manufacturers, Inc.: 7.____

Sales	$1,000.000
Sales Returns	95,000

Cost of Sales	
Opening Inventories	$200,000
Purchases During the Year	567,000
Direct Labor Costs	240,000
Factory Overhead	24,400
Inventories End of Year	235,000

On June 5, 2021, a fire destroyed the plant and all of the inventories then on hand. You are given the following information and asked to ascertain the amount of the estimated inventory loss.

Sales up to June 15	$545,000
Purchased to June 15	254,500
Direct Labor	233,000
Overhead	14,550
Salvaged Inventory	95,000

The ESTIMATED inventory loss is
A. $96,000 B. $162,450 C. $189,450 D. $257,450

8. Losses and excessive costs with regard to inventory can occur in any one of several operating functions of an organization. 8.____
The operating function which bears the GREATEST responsibility for the failure to give proper consideration to transportation costs of material acquisitions is
A. accounting B. purchasing C. receiving D. shipping

Questions 9-17.

DIRECTIONS: Questions 9 through 17 are to be answered on the basis of the following information.

You are conducting an audit of the PAP Company, which has a contract to supply the municipal hospitals with specialty refrigerators on a cost-plus basis. The following information is available:

Materials Purchased	$1,946,700
Inventories, January 1	
Materials	268,000
Finished Goods (100 units)	43,000
Direct Labor	2,125,800
Factory Overhead (40% variable)	764,000
Marketing Expenses (all fixed)	516,000
Administrative Expenses (all fixed)	461,000
Sales (12,400 units)	6,634,000
Inventories, March 31	
Materials	167,000
Finished Goods (200 units)	(omitted)
No Work in Process	

9. The NET INCOME for the period is 9.____
A. $755,500 B. $1,237,500 C. $1,732,500 D. $4,980,500

10. The number of units manufactured is 10.____
A. 12,400 B. 12,500 C. 12,600 D. 12,700

11. The unit cost of refrigerators manufactured is MOST NEARLY 11.____
A. $389.00 B. $395.00 C. $398.00 D. $400.00

12. The TOTAL variable costs are 12.____
A. $305,600 B. $464,000 C. $4,479,100 D. $4,937,500

13. The TOTAL fixed costs are 13.____
A. $458,400 B. $1,435,400 C. $1,471,800 D. $1,741,000

While you are conducting your audit, the PAP Company advises you that they have changed their inventory costing from FIFO to LIFO. You are interested in pursuing the matter further because this change will affect the cost of the refrigerators. An examination of material part 2-317 inventory card shows the following activity:

May 2 – Received 100 units @ $5.40 per unit
May 8 – Received 30 units @ $8.00 per unit
May 15 – Issued 50 units
May 22 – Received 120 units @ $9.00 per unit
May 29 – Issued 100 units

14. Using the FIFO method under a perpetual inventory control system, the TOTAL cost of the units issued in May is   14.____
    A. $690   B. $960   C. $1,590   D. $1,860

15. Using the FIFO method under a perpetual inventory control system, the VALUE of the closing inventory is   15.____
    A. $780   B. $900   C. $1,080   D. $1,590

16. Using the LIFO method under a perpetual inventory control system, the TOTAL cost of the units issued in May is   16.____
    A. $1,248   B. $1,428   C. $1,720   D. $1,860

17. Using the LIFO method under a perpetual inventory control system, the value of the closing inventory is   17.____
    A. $612   B. $380   C. $1,512   D. $1,680

Questions 18-20.

DIRECTIONS: For Questions 18 through 20, consider that the EEF Corporation has a fully integrated cost accounting system.

18. Unit cost of manufacturing dresses was $7.00. Spoiled dresses numbered 400 with a sales value of $800.
    When it is not customary to have a Spoiled Work account, the MOST appropriate account to be credited is   18.____
    A. Work in Process   B. Cost of Sales
    C. Manufacturing Overhead   D. Finished Goods

19. Overtime premium for factory workers (direct labor) totaled $400 for the payroll period. This was due to inadequate plant capacity.
    The account to be DEBITED is   19.____
    A. Work in Process   B. Cost of Sales
    C. Manufacturing Overhead   D. Finished Goods

20. A month-end physical inventory of stores shows a shortage of $175. The account to be DEBITED to correct this shortage is

20.____

A. Stores
B. Work in Process
C. Cost of Sales
D. Manufacturing Overhead

KEY (CORRECT ANSWERS)

1.	A	11.	B
2.	A	12.	C
3.	C	13.	B
4.	C	14.	B
5.	A	15.	B
6.	D	16.	A
7.	B	17.	A
8.	B	18.	A
9.	A	19.	C
10.	B	20.	C

EXAMINATION SECTION
TEST 1

DIRECTIONS: Each question or incomplete statement is followed by several suggested answers or completions. Select the one that BEST answers the question or completes the statement. *PRINT THE LETTER OF THE CORRECT ANSWER IN THE SPACE AT THE RIGHT.*

1. In a statement of support, revenue, and expenses and changes in fund balances of a voluntary health and welfare organization, depreciation expense should 1.____

   A. not be included
   B. be included as an element of support
   C. be included as an element of other changes in fund balances
   D. be included as an element of expense

2. Which of the following NORMALLY would be included in Other Operating Revenues of a hospital? 2.____

	Revenue from educational programs	Unrestricted gifts
A.	Yes	No
B.	Yes	Yes
C.	No	Yes
D.	No	No

3. In the comprehensive annual financial report (CAFR) of a governmental unit, the account groups are included in 3.____

   A. both the combined balance sheet and the combined statement of revenues, expenditures, and changes in fund balances
   B. the combined statement of revenues, expenditures, and changes in fund balances, but not the combined balance sheet
   C. the combined balance sheet but not the combined statement of revenues, expenditures, and changes in fund balances
   D. neither the combined balance sheet nor the combined statement of revenues, expenditures, and changes in fund balances

4. Funds which the governing board of an institution, rather than a donor or other outside agency, has determined are to be retained and invested for other than loan or plant purposes would be accounted for in the 4.____

   A. quasi-endowment fund
   B. endowment fund
   C. agency fund
   D. current fund-restricted

5. Which of the following accounts would be included in the fund equity section of the combined balance sheet of a governmental unit for the general fixed asset account group? 5.____

	Investment in general fixed assets	Fund balance reserved for encumbrances
A.	Yes	Yes
B.	Yes	No
C.	No	No
D.	No	Yes

6. Which of the following funds of a governmental unit would account for depreciation in the accounts of the fund? 6.____

   A. General
   B. Internal service
   C. Capital projects
   D. Special assessment

7. Which of the following funds of a governmental unit uses the modified accrual basis of accounting? 7.____

   A. Enterprise
   B. Internal service
   C. Capital projects
   D. Nonexpendable trust

8. The expenditures control account of a governmental unit is credited when 8.____

   A. the budgetary accounts are closed
   B. the budget is recorded
   C. supplies are purchased
   D. supplies previously encumbered are received

9. The appropriations control account of a governmental unit is credited when 9.____

   A. supplies are purchased
   B. expenditures are recorded
   C. the budget is recorded
   D. the budgetary accounts are closed

10. Under the modified accrual basis of accounting for a governmental unit, revenues should be recognized in the accounting period in which they 10.____

   A. are earned and become measurable
   B. are collected
   C. become available and earned
   D. become available and measurable

11. How would the following be used in the economic order quantity formula? 11.____

	Inventory carrying cost	Cost per purchase order
A.	Numerator	Numerator
B.	Denominator	Numerator
C.	Denominator	Denominator
D.	Not used	Denominator

12. A company's rate of return on investment is the ______ by the capital-employed turnover rate. 12.____

   A. percentage of profit to sales divided
   B. percentage of profit to sales multiplied
   C. investment capital divided
   D. investment capital multiplied

13. A proposed project has an expected economic life of eight years. In the calculation of the net present value of the proposed project, salvage value would be — 13._____

A. excluded from the calculation of the net present value
B. included as a cash inflow at the estimated salvage value
C. included as a cash inflow at the future amount of the estimated salvage value
D. included as a cash inflow at the present value of the estimated salvage value

14. Breakeven analysis assumes over the relevant range that — 14._____

A. total costs are linear
B. fixed costs are nonlinear
C. variable costs are nonlinear
D. selling prices are nonlinear

15. The flexible budget for a producing department may include — 15._____

	Direct labor	Factory overhead
A.	No	Yes
B.	No	No
C.	Yes	No
D.	Yes	Yes

16. In an income statement prepared as an internal report using the absorption costing method, which of the following terms should appear? — 16._____

	Contribution margin	Gross profit (margin)
A.	No	Yes
B.	No	No
C.	Yes	No
D.	Yes	Yes

17. For the purposes of cost accumulation, which of the following are identifiable as different individual products before the split-off point? — 17._____

	Byproducts	Joint products
A.	Yes	Yes
B.	Yes	No
C.	No	No
D.	No	Yes

18. Under the two-variance method for analyzing factory overhead, the factory overhead applied to production is used in the computation of the — 18._____

	Controllable (budget) variance	Volume variance
A.	Yes	No
B.	Yes	Yes
C.	No	Yes
D.	No	No

19. In a job order cost system, direct labor costs USUALLY are recorded initially as an increase in — 19._____

A. factory overhead applied
B. factory overhead control
C. finished goods control
D. work in process control

20. In developing a factory overhead application rate for use in a process costing system, which of the following could be used in the denominator? 20.____

A. Estimated direct labor hours
B. Actual direct labor hours
C. Estimated factory overhead
D. Actual factory overhead

21. How are dividends per share for common stock used in the calculation of the following? 21.____

	Dividend per-share payout ratio	Earnings per share
A.	Numerator	Numerator
B.	Numerator	Not used
C.	Denominator	Not used
D.	Denominator	Denominator

22. An employer sponsoring a defined benefit pension plan should disclose the 22.____

	Amount of unrecognized prior service cost	Fair value of plan assets
A.	No	No
B.	No	Yes
C.	Yes	Yes
D.	Yes	No

23. An investment in marketable securities was accounted for by the cost method. These securities were distributed to stockholders as a property dividend in a nonreciprocal transfer. 23.____
The dividend should be reported at the

A. fair value of the asset transferred
B. fair value of the asset transferred or the recorded amount of the asset transferred, whichever is higher
C. fair value of the asset transferred or the recorded amount of the asset transferred, whichever is lower
D. recorded amount of the asset transferred

24. A development stage enterprise 24.____

A. issues an income statement that is the same as an established operating enterprise, and shows cumulative amounts from the enterprise's inception as additional information
B. issues an income statement that is the same as an established operating enterprise, but does not show cumulative amounts from the enterprise's inception as additional information
C. issues an income statement that only shows cumulative amounts from the enterprise's inception
D. does not issue an income statement

25. An inventory loss from a market price decline occurred in the first quarter. The loss was not expected to be restored in the fiscal year. However, in the third quarter the inventory had a market price recovery that exceeded the market decline that occurred in the first quarter.
For interim financial reporting, the dollar amount of net inventory should

25.____

A. decrease in the first quarter by the amount of the market price decline and increase in the third quarter by the amount of the market price recovery
B. decrease in the first quarter by the amount of the market price decline and increase in the third quarter by the amount of decrease in the first quarter
C. not be affected in the first quarter and increase in the third quarter by the amount of the market price recovery that exceeded the amount of the market price decline
D. not be affected in either the first quarter or the third quarter

26. When Dubke retired from the partnership of Dubke, Logan and Flaherty, the final settlement of Dubke's partnership interest exceeded Dubke's capital balance.
Under the bonus method, the excess

26.____

A. was recorded as goodwill
B. was recorded as an expense
C. had no effect on the capital balances of Logan and Flaherty
D. reduced the capital balances of Logan and Flaherty

27. A company issued rights to its existing shareholders to purchase, for $30 per share, unissued shares of $15 par value common stock.
Additional paid-in capital will be credited when the

27.____

	Rights are issued	Rights lapse
A.	Yes	No
B.	No	No
C.	No	Yes
D.	Yes	Yes

28. Five thousand (5,000) shares of common stock with a par value of $10 per share were issued initially at $12 per share. Subsequently, one thousand (1,000) of these shares were acquired as treasury stock at $15 per share. Assuming that the par value method of accounting for treasury stock transactions is used, what is the effect of the acquisition of the treasury stock on each of the following?

28.____

	Additional paid-in capital	Retained earnings
A.	Increase	No effect
B.	Increase	Decrease
C.	Decrease	Increase
D.	Decrease	Decrease

29. In determining primary earnings per share, a common stock equivalent was antidilutive in 2015 and dilutive in 2016.
The common stock equivalent would be included in the computation for

29.____

	2015	2016
A.	Yes	Yes
B.	No	Yes
C.	No	No
D.	Yes	No

30. The deferred method of tax allocation should be used for 30.____

	Permanent differences	Timing differences
A.	Yes	No
B.	Yes	Yes
C.	No	Yes
D.	No	No

KEY (CORRECT ANSWERS)

1. D
2. A
3. C
4. A
5. B
6. B
7. C
8. A
9. C
10. D
11. B
12. B
13. D
14. A
15. D
16. A
17. C
18. C
19. D
20. A
21. B
22. C
23. A
24. A
25. B
26. D
27. B
28. D
29. B
30. C

TEST 2

DIRECTIONS: Each question or incomplete statement is followed by several suggested answers or completions. Select the one that BEST answers the question or completes the statement. *PRINT THE LETTER OF THE CORRECT ANSWER IN THE SPACE AT THE RIGHT.*

1. When a company changes the expected service life of an asset because additional information has been obtained, which of the following should be reported? 1.____

	Cumulative effect of change in accounting principle	Pro forma effects of retroactive application
A.	Yes	No
B.	Yes	Yes
C.	No	Yes
D.	No	No

2. Which of the following should be presented in a statement of changes in financial position prepared on a cash basis? 2.____

	Stock dividend	Stock split
A.	Yes	Yes
B.	Yes	No
C.	No	No
D.	No	Yes

3. In a statement of changes in financial position prepared on a cash basis (indirect method), an increase in inventories should be presented as a(n) 3.____

   A. outflow of cash
   B. inflow and outflow of cash
   C. addition to income from continuing operations
   D. deduction from income from continuing operations

4. A lease is recorded as a sales-type lease by the lessor. The difference between the gross investment in the lease and the sum of the present values of the two components of the gross investment (the net receivable) should be 4.____

   A. amortized over the period of the lease as interest revenue using the interest method
   B. amortized over the period of the lease as interest revenue using the straight-line method
   C. recognized in full as interest revenue at the lease's inception
   D. recognized in full as manufacturer's or dealer's profit at the lease's inception

5. A company uses the percentage-of-completion method to account for a four-year construction contract. 5.____
   Progress billings sent in the second year that were collected in the third year would ______ included in the calculation of the income recognized in the ______ year.

   A. not be; second, third, or fourth
   B. be; second
   C. be; third
   D. be; fourth

6. A material loss should be presented separately as a component of income from continuing operations when it is — 6.____

   A. infrequent in occurrence and unusual in nature
   B. infrequent in occurrence but not unusual in nature
   C. a cumulative effect-type change in accounting principle
   D. an extraordinary item

7. A December 15, 2015, purchase of goods was denominated in a currency other than the entity's functional currency. The transaction resulted in a payable that was fixed in terms of the amount of foreign currency and was paid on the settlement date, January 20, 2016.
   The exchange rates between the functional currency and the currency in which the transaction was denominated changed at December 31, 2015, resulting in a loss that should — 7.____

   A. not be reported until January 20, 2016, the settlement date
   B. be included as a separate component of stockholders' equity at December 31, 2015
   C. be included as a deferred charge at December 31, 2015
   D. be included as a component of income from continuing operations for 2015

8. Which of the following components should be included in the calculation of net pension cost recognized for a period by an employer sponsoring a defined benefit pension plan? — 8.____

	Actual return on plan assets if any	Amortization of unrecognized prior service cost, if any
A.	No	Yes
B.	No	No
C.	Yes	No
D.	Yes	Yes

9. When the interest payment dates of a bond are May 1 and November 1, and the bond is issued on June 1, 2015, the amount of interest expense for the year ended December 31, 2015 would be for ______ months. — 9.____

   A. two B. six C. seven D. eight

10. How would retained earnings be affected by the declaration of each of the following? — 10.____

	Stock dividend	Stock split
A.	Decrease	Decrease
B.	No effect	Decrease
C.	No effect	No effect
D.	Decrease	No effect

11. A company declared a cash dividend on its common stock in December 2015, payable in January 2016.
    Retained earnings would — 11.____

    A. increase on the date of declaration
    B. not be affected on the date of declaration
    C. not be affected on the date of payment
    D. decrease on the date of payment

12. A safety hazard exists for a manufactured product. 12.____
Occurrence of the loss is reasonably possible, and the amount of the loss can be reasonably estimated.
This loss contingency should be

	Accrued	Disclosed
A.	Yes	Yes
B.	Yes	No
C.	No	Yes
D.	No	No

13. The proceeds from a bond issued with detachable stock purchase warrants should be accounted for 13.____

A. entirely as bonds payable
B. entirely as stockholders' equity
C. partially as unearned revenue and partially as bonds payable
D. partially as stockholders' equity and partially as bonds payable

14. A five-year term bond was issued by a company on January 1, 2015 at a premium. 14.____
The carrying amount of the bond at December 31, 2016 would be

A. the same as the carrying amount at January 1, 2015
B. higher than the carrying amount at December 31, 2015
C. lower than the carrying amount at December 31, 2017
D. lower than the carrying amount at December 31, 2015

15. The market price of a bond issued at a discount is the present value of its principal amount at the market (effective) rate of interest 15.____

A. plus the present value of all future interest payments at the market (effective) rate of interest
B. plus the present value of all future interest payments at the rate of interest stated on the bond
C. less the present value of all future interest payments at the market (effective) rate of interest
D. less the present value of all future interest payments at the rate of interest stated on the bond

16. At the most recent year-end, a company had a deferred income tax credit related to a noncurrent asset that exceeded a deferred income tax charge related to a current liability. 16.____
Which of the following should be reported in the company's most recent year-end balance sheet?

A. The excess of the deferred income tax credit over the deferred income tax charge as a noncurrent liability
B. The excess of the deferred income tax credit over the deferred income tax charge as a current liability
C. The deferred income tax credit as a noncurrent liability
D. The deferred income tax credit as a current liability

17. Lease Y does not contain a bargain purchase option, but the lease term is equal to 90 percent of the estimated economic life of the leased property. Lease Z does not transfer ownership of the property to the lessee by the end of the lease term, but the lease term is equal to 75 percent of the estimated economic life of the leased property. How should the lessee classify these leases?

17.____

	Lease Y	Lease Z
A.	Capital lease	Operating lease
B.	Capital lease	Capital lease
C.	Operating lease	Capital lease
D.	Operating lease	Operating lease

18. A six-year capital lease specifies equal minimum annual lease payments. Part of this payment represents interest and part represents a reduction in the net lease liability. The portion of the minimum lease payment in the fourth year applicable to the reduction of the net lease liability should be

18.____

A. the same as in the third year
B. less than in the third year
C. less than in the fifth year
D. more than in the fifth year

19. A retail store received cash and issued gift certificates that are redeemable in merchandise. The gift certificates lapse one year after they are issued. How would the deferred revenue account be affected by each of the following transactions?

19.____

	Redemption of certificates	Lapse of certificates
A.	No effect	Decrease
B.	Decrease	Decrease
C.	Decrease	No effect
D.	No effect	No effect

20. Which of the following is classified as an accrued liability?

20.____

	Liability for federal unemployment taxes	Liability for employer's share of FICA taxes
A.	Yes	Yes
B.	Yes	No
C.	No	No
D.	No	Yes

21. A company borrowed cash from a bank and issued to the bank a short-term noninterest-bearing note payable. The bank discounted the note at 10% and remitted the proceeds to the company. The effective interest rate-paid by the company in this transaction would be _______ the stated discount rate of 10%

21.____

A. equal to
B. more than
C. less than
D. independent of

22. The premium on a three-year insurance policy expiring on December 31, 2017 was paid in total on January 1, 2015. The original payment was initially debited to a prepaid asset account. The appropriate journal entry has been recorded on December 31, 2015. The balance in the prepaid asset account on December 31, 2015 should be 22.____

A. zero
B. the same as it would have been if the original payment had been debited initially to an expense account
C. the same as the original payment
D. higher than if the original payment had been debited initially to an expense account

23. The market price of the common stock of an investee company increased during the year. How will the investor's investment account be affected by the increase in market price of that common stock under each of the following accounting methods? 23.____

	Cost method	Equity method
A,	No effect	No effect
B.	No effect	Increase
C.	Increase	No effect
D.	Increase	Increase

24. An investor purchased a bond classified as a long-term investment between interest dates at a discount. At the purchase date, the carrying amount of the bond is more than the 24.____

	Cash paid to seller	Face amount of bond
A.	Yes	No
B.	Yes	Yes
C.	No	Yes
D.	No	No

25. When the market value of an investment in debt securities exceeds its carrying amount, how should the asset be reported at the end of the year for each of the following? 25.____

	Short-term marketable debt securities	Long-term marketable debt securities
A.	Carrying amount	Market
B.	Carrying amount	Carrying amount
C.	Market	Carrying amount
D.	Market	Market

26. A marketable equity securities portfolio is included in an unclassified balance sheet. The amount by which the aggregate cost of the marketable equity securities portfolio exceeds its aggregate market value should 26.____

A. be reported as a valuation allowance in the asset section of the balance sheet
B. be reported as a valuation allowance in the liability section of the balance sheet
C. be reported as an unrealized loss in the income statement
D. not be reported in the financial statements

27. When the allowance method of recognizing bad debt expense is used, the allowance for doubtful accounts would decrease when a(n) 27.____

    A. specific account receivable is collected
    B. account previously written off is collected
    C. account previously written off becomes collectible
    D. specific uncollectible account is written off

28. On July 1, 2015, a company received a one-year note receivable bearing interest at the market rate. The face amount of the note receivable and the entire amount of the interest are due on June 30, 2016. 28.____
    The interest receivable account would show a balance on

    A. July 1, 2015 but not December 31, 2015
    B. December 31, 2015 but not July 1, 2015
    C. July 1, 2015 and December 31, 2015
    D. neither July 1, 2015 nor December 31, 2015

29. When purchasing power gains or losses are computed, how is each of the following classified? 29.____

	Patents	Unamortized premium on bonds payable
A.	Nonmonetary	Monetary
B.	Nonmonetary	Nonmonetary
C.	Monetary	Nonmonetary
D.	Monetary	Monetary

30. According to the FASB conceptual framework, predictive value is an ingredient of 30.____

	Relevance	Reliability
A.	Yes	No
B.	Yes	Yes
C.	No	Yes
D.	No	No

KEY (CORRECT ANSWERS)

1. D
2. C
3. D
4. A
5. A

6. B
7. D
8. D
9. C
10. D

11. C
12. C
13. D
14. D
15. A

16. C
17. B
18. C
19. B
20. A

21. B
22. B
23. A
24. D
25. B

26. A
27. D
28. B
29. A
30. A

EXAMINATION SECTION
TEST 1

DIRECTIONS: Each question or incomplete statement is followed by several suggested answers or completions. Select the one that BEST answers the question or completes the statement. *PRINT THE LETTER OF THE CORRECT ANSWER IN THE SPACE AT THE RIGHT.*

1. If an auditor believes there is minimal likelihood that resolution of an uncertainty will have a material effect on the financial statements, the auditor should issue a(n) _______ opinion. 1.____

   A. unqualified
   B. disclaimer of
   C. *except for* qualified
   D. *subject to* qualified

2. Which of the following BEST describes the auditor's reporting responsibility concerning information accompanying the basic financial statements in an auditor-submitted document? 2.____
   The auditor should report on

   A. all the information included in the document
   B. the basic financial statements but may not issue a report covering the accompanying information
   C. the information accompanying the basic financial statements only if the auditor participated in the preparation of the accompanying information
   D. the information accompanying the basic financial statements only if the document is being distributed to public shareholders

3. Which of the following are prospective financial statements upon which an accountant may appropriately report for general use? 3.____

   A. Pro forma financial statements
   B. Financial projections
   C. Partial presentations
   D. Financial forecasts

4. Given one or more hypothetical assumptions, a responsible party may prepare, to the best of its knowledge and belief, an entity's expected financial position, results of operations, and changes in financial position. 4.____
   Such prospective financial statements are known as

   A. Pro forma financial statements
   B. Financial projections
   C. Partial presentations
   D. Financial forecasts

5. Subsequent to the issuance of the auditor's report, the auditor became aware of facts existing at the report date that would have affected the report had the auditor then been aware of such facts. 5.____
   After determining that the information is reliable, the auditor should NEXT

A. notify the board of directors that the auditor's report must no longer be associated with the financial statements
B. determine whether there are persons relying or likely to rely on the financial statements who would attach importance to the information
C. request that management disclose the effects of the newly discovered information by adding a footnote to subsequently issued financial statements
D. issue revised pro forma financial statements taking into consideration the newly discovered information

6. When an auditor reports on financial statements prepared on an entity's income tax basis, the auditor's report should 6._____

A. disclose that the statements are not intended to conform with generally accepted accounting principles
B. disclaim an opinion on whether the statements were examined in accordance with generally accepted auditing standards
C. not express an opinion on whether the statements are presented in conformity with the comprehensive basis of accounting used
D. include an explanation of how the results of operations differ from the cash receipts and disbursements basis of accounting

7. When reporting on comparative financial statements where the financial statements of the prior period have been examined by a predecessor auditor whose report is not presented, the successor auditor should indicate in the scope paragraph 7._____

A. the reasons why the predecessor auditor's report is not presented
B. the identity of the predecessor auditor who examined the financial statements of the prior year
C. whether the predecessor auditor's review of the current year's financial statements revealed any matters that might have a material effect on the successor auditor's opinion
D. the type of opinion expressed by the predecessor auditor

8. The auditor would MOST likely issue a disclaimer of opinion because of 8._____

A. the client's failure to present supplementary information required by the FASB
B. inadequate disclosure of material information
C. a client imposed scope limitation
D. the qualification of an opinion by the other auditor of a subsidiary where there is a division of responsibility

9. The principal auditor is satisfied with the independence and professional reputation of the other auditor who has audited a subsidiary but wants to indicate the division of responsibility.
The principal auditor should 9._____

A. modify only the scope paragraph of the report
B. modify only the opinion paragraph of the report
C. modify both the scope and opinion paragraphs of the report
D. not modify the report except for inclusion of a separate explanatory paragraph

10. The management of a client company believes that the statement of changes in financial position (statement of cash flows) is not a useful document and refuses to include one in the annual report to stockholders. 10.____
As a result of this circumstance, the auditor's opinion should be

    A. adverse
    B. unqualified
    C. qualified due to inadequate disclosure
    D. qualified due to a scope limitation

11. When an auditor qualifies an opinion because of a scope limitation, which paragraph(s) of the auditor's report should indicate that the qualification pertains to the possible effects on the financial statements and not to the scope limitation itself? 11.____

    A. The scope paragraph and the separate explanatory paragraph
    B. The separate explanatory paragraph and the opinion paragraph
    C. The scope paragraph *only*
    D. The opinion paragraph *only*

12. When an independent accountant's report based on a review of interim financial information is incorporated by reference in a registration statement, the Securities and Exchange Commission requires that the prospectus clarify that the accountant's report is NOT 12.____

    A. a part of the registration statement within the meaning of the Securities Act of 1933
    B. subject to the Statements on Standards for Accounting and Review Services
    C. to be relied upon due to the limited nature of the procedures applied
    D. included in the company's quarterly report on Form 10-Q

13. A client acquired 25% of its outstanding capital stock after year-end and prior to completion of the auditor's field work. 13.____
The auditor should

    A. advise management to adjust the balance sheet to reflect the acquisition
    B. issue pro forma financial statements giving effect to the acquisition as if it had occurred at year-end
    C. advise management to disclose the acquisition in the notes to the financial statements
    D. disclose the acquisition in the opinion paragraph of the auditor's report

14. An auditor concludes that an audit procedure considered necessary at the time of the examination had been omitted. The auditor should assess the importance of the omitted procedure to the ability to support the previously expressed opinion. 14.____
Which of the following would be LEAST helpful in making that assessment?

    A. A discussion with the client about whether there are persons relying on the auditor's report
    B. A reevaluation of the overall scope of the examination
    C. A discussion of the circumstances with engagement personnel
    D. A review of the other audit procedures that were applied that might compensate for the one omitted

15. Which of the following statements concerning the auditor's use of the work of a specialist is CORRECT? 15.____

    A. If the specialist is related to the client, the auditor is not permitted to use the specialist's findings as corroborative evidence.
    B. The specialist may be identified in the auditor's report only when the auditor issues a qualified opinion.
    C. The specialist should have an understanding of the auditor's corroborative use of the specialist's findings.
    D. If the auditor believes that the determinations made by the specialist are unreasonable, only an adverse opinion may be issued.

16. When using a computer to gather evidence, the auditor need not have working knowledge of the client's programming language. 16.____
    However, it is necessary that the auditor understand the

    A. audit specifications
    B. programming techniques
    C. database retrieval system
    D. manual testing techniques

17. Which of the following is NOT a major reason why an accounting audit trail should be maintained for a computer system? 17.____

    A. Query answering
    B. Deterrent to irregularities
    C. Monitoring purposes
    D. Analytical review

18. Working papers that record the procedures used by the auditor to gather evidence should be 18.____

    A. considered the primary support for the financial statements being examined
    B. viewed as the connecting link between the books of account and the financial statements
    C. designed to meet the circumstances of the particular engagement
    D. destroyed when the audited entity ceases to be a client

19. If the financial statements, including accompanying notes, fail to disclose information that is required by generally accepted accounting principles, the auditor should express either a(n) 19.____

    A. *except for* qualified opinion or an adverse opinion
    B. adverse opinion or a *subject to* qualified opinion
    C. *subject to* qualified opinion or an unqualified opinion with a separate explanatory paragraph
    D. unqualified opinion with a separate explanatory paragraph or an *except for* qualified opinion

20. If there were no changes during the reporting period in the application of accounting principles, which of the following types of opinions should omit any reference to consistency? 20.____
    ______ opinion.

    A. *except for* qualified
    B. unqualified
    C. *subject to* qualified
    D. adverse

21. A limitation on the scope of the auditor's examination sufficient to preclude an unqualified opinion will ALWAYS result when management 21.____

    A. prevents the auditor from reviewing the working papers of the predecessor auditor
    B. engages the auditor after the year-end physical inventory count is completed
    C. fails to correct a material internal accounting control weakness that had been identified during the prior year's audit
    D. refuses to furnish a management representation letter to the auditor

22. Operational auditing is PRIMARILY oriented toward 22.____

    A. future improvements to accomplish the goals of management
    B. the accuracy of data reflected in management's financial records
    C. the verification that a company's financial statements are fairly presented
    D. past protection provided by existing internal accounting control

23. Which of the following is the BEST audit procedure for determining the existence of unrecorded liabilities at year-end? 23.____
    Examine

    A. a sample of invoices dated a few days prior to and subsequent to year-end to ascertain whether they have been properly recorded
    B. a sample of cash disbursements in the period subsequent to year-end
    C. confirmation requests returned by creditors whose accounts appear on a subsidiary trial balance of accounts payable
    D. unusual relationships between monthly accounts payable balances and recorded purchases

24. An auditor ordinarily should send a standard confirmation request to all banks with which the client has done business during the year under audit, regardless of the year-end balance, because this procedure 24.____

    A. provides for confirmation regarding compensating balance arrangements
    B. detects kiting activities that may otherwise not be discovered
    C. seeks information about indebtedness to the bank
    D. verifies securities held by the bank in safekeeping

25. On receiving the bank cutoff statement, the auditor should trace 25.____

    A. deposits in transit on the year-end bank reconciliation to deposits in the cash receipts journal
    B. checks dated prior to year-end to the outstanding checks listed on the year-end bank reconciliation
    C. deposits listed on the cutoff statement to deposits in the cash receipts journal
    D. checks dated subsequent to year-end to the outstanding checks listed on the year-end bank reconciliations

26. Which of the following would the accountant MOST likely investigate during the review of financial statements of a nonpublic entity if accounts receivable did not conform to a predictable pattern during the year? 26.____

    A. Sales returns and allowances
    B. Credit sales
    C. Sales of consigned goods
    D. Cash sales

27. Prior to commencing the compilation of financial statements of a nonpublic entity, the accountant should 27.____

    A. perform analytical review procedures sufficient to determine whether fluctuations among account balances appear reasonable
    B. complete the preliminary phase of the study and evaluation of the entity's internal accounting control
    C. verify that the financial information supplied by the entity agrees with the books of original entry
    D. acquire a knowledge of any specialized accounting principles and practices used in the entity's industry

28. After discovering that a related party transaction exists, the auditor should be aware that the 28.____

    A. substance of the transaction could be significantly different from its form
    B. adequacy of disclosure of the transaction is secondary to its legal form
    C. transaction is assumed to be outside the ordinary course of business
    D. financial statements should recognize the legal form of the transaction rather than its substance

29. Which of the following auditing procedures is ordinarily performed LAST? 29.____

    A. Obtaining a management representation letter
    B. Testing the purchasing function
    C. Reading the minutes of directors' meetings
    D. Confirming accounts payable

30. Which of the following is the MOST effective audit procedure for verification of dividends earned on investments in marketable equity securities? 30.____

    A. Tracing deposit of dividend checks to the cash receipts book
    B. Reconciling amounts received with published dividend records
    C. Comparing the amounts received with preceding year dividends received
    D. Recomputing selected extensions and footings of dividend schedules and comparing totals to the general ledger

KEY (CORRECT ANSWERS)

1. A
2. A
3. D
4. B
5. B

6. A
7. D
8. C
9. C
10. C

11. D
12. A
13. C
14. A
15. C

16. A
17. D
18. C
19. A
20. D

21. D
22. A
23. B
24. C
25. B

26. B
27. D
28. A
29. A
30. B

TEST 2

DIRECTIONS: Each question or incomplete statement is followed by several suggested answers or completions. Select the one that BEST answers the question or completes the statement. *PRINT THE LETTER OF THE CORRECT ANSWER IN THE SPACE AT THE RIGHT.*

1. When auditing merchandise inventory at year-end, the auditor performs a purchase cut-off test to obtain evidence that 1.____

   A. all goods purchased before year-end are received before the physical inventory count
   B. no goods held on consignment for customers are included in the inventory balance
   C. no goods observed during the physical count are pledged or sold
   D. all goods owned at year-end are included in the inventory balance

2. Without the consent of the client, a CPA should NOT disclose confidential client information contained in working papers to a 2.____

   A. voluntary quality control review board
   B. CPA firm that has purchased the CPA's accounting practice
   C. federal court that has issued a valid subpoena
   D. disciplinary body created under state statute

3. An example of an analytical review procedure is the comparison of 3.____

   A. financial information with similar information regarding the industry in which the entity operates
   B. recorded amounts of major disbursements with appropriate invoices
   C. results of a statistical sample with the expected characteristics of the actual population
   D. EDP generated data with similar data generated by a manual accounting system

4. Audit evidence can come in different forms with different degrees of persuasiveness. Which of the following is the LEAST persuasive type of evidence? 4.____

   A. Bank statement obtained from the client
   B. Computations made by the auditor
   C. Prenumbered client sales invoices
   D. Vendor's invoice

Questions 5-7.

DIRECTIONS: Questions 5 through 7 are to be answered on the basis of the following section of a system flowchart for a payroll application.

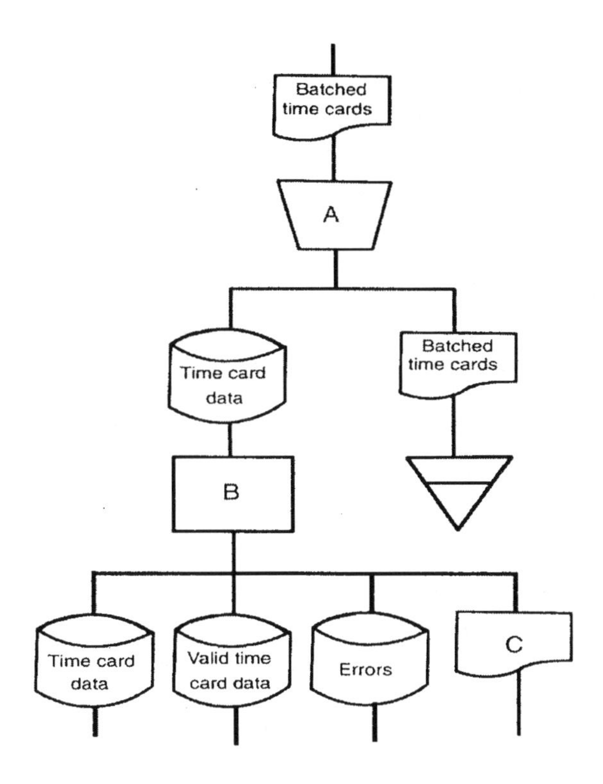

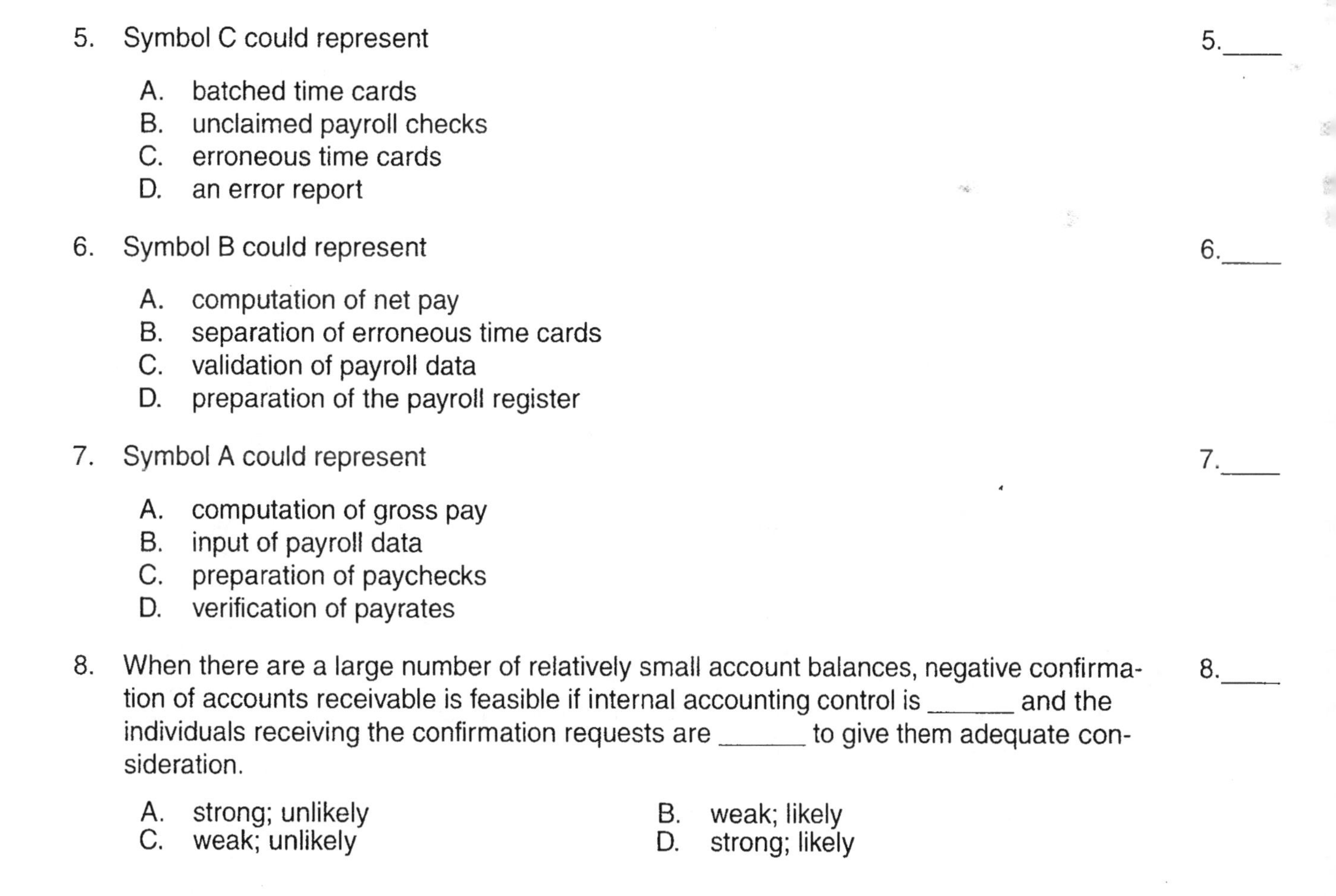

5. Symbol C could represent   5.____

   A. batched time cards
   B. unclaimed payroll checks
   C. erroneous time cards
   D. an error report

6. Symbol B could represent   6.____

   A. computation of net pay
   B. separation of erroneous time cards
   C. validation of payroll data
   D. preparation of the payroll register

7. Symbol A could represent   7.____

   A. computation of gross pay
   B. input of payroll data
   C. preparation of paychecks
   D. verification of payrates

8. When there are a large number of relatively small account balances, negative confirmation of accounts receivable is feasible if internal accounting control is ______ and the individuals receiving the confirmation requests are ______ to give them adequate consideration.   8.____

   A. strong; unlikely
   B. weak; likely
   C. weak; unlikely
   D. strong; likely

9. When there are few property and equipment transactions during the year, the continuing auditor USUALLY makes a 9.____

   A. complete review of the related internal accounting controls and performs compliance tests of those controls being relied upon
   B. complete review of the related internal accounting controls and performs analytical review tests to verify current year additions to property and equipment
   C. preliminary review of the related internal accounting controls and performs a thorough examination of the balances at the beginning of the year
   D. preliminary review of the related internal accounting controls and performs extensive tests of current year property and equipment transactions

10. A weakness in internal accounting control over recording retirements of equipment may cause the auditor to 10.____

   A. inspect certain items of equipment in the plant and trace those items to the accounting records
   B. review the subsidiary ledger to ascertain whether depreciation was taken on each item of equipment during the year
   C. trace additions to the *other assets* account to search for equipment that is still on hand but no longer being used
   D. select certain items of equipment from the accounting records and locate them in the plant

11. The auditor may observe the distribution of paychecks to ascertain whether 11.____

   A. payrate authorization is properly separated from the operating function
   B. deductions from gross pay are calculated correctly and are properly authorized
   C. employees of record actually exist and are employed by the client
   D. paychecks agree with the payroll register and the time cards

12. The auditor's communication of material weaknesses in internal accounting control is 12.____

   A. required to enable the auditor to state that the examination has been made in accordance with generally accepted auditing standards
   B. the principal reason for studying and evaluating the system of internal accounting controls
   C. incident to the auditor's objective of forming an opinion as to the fair presentation of the financial statements
   D. required to be documented in a written report to the board of directors or the board's audit committee

13. The purpose of segregating the duties of hiring personnel and distributing payroll checks is to separate the 13.____

   A. operational responsibility from the record keeping responsibility
   B. responsibilities of recording a transaction at its origin from the ultimate posting in the general ledger
   C. authorization of transactions from the custody of related assets
   D. human resources function from the controllership function

14. Which of the following internal accounting control procedures could BEST prevent direct labor from being charged to manufacturing overhead? 14.____

    A. Reconciliation of work in process inventory with cost records
    B. Comparison of daily journal entries with factory labor summary
    C. Comparison of periodic cost budgets and time cards
    D. Reconciliation of unfinished job summary and production cost records

15. Instead of taking a physical inventory count on the balance-sheet date, the client may take physical counts prior to the year-end if internal accounting controls are adequate and 15.____

    A. computerized records of perpetual inventory are maintained
    B. inventory is slow-moving
    C. EDP error reports are generated for missing pre-numbered inventory tickets
    D. obsolete inventory items are segregated and excluded

16. In a properly designed internal accounting control system, the same employee may be permitted to 16.____

    A. receive and deposit checks, and also approve writeoffs of customer accounts
    B. approve vouchers for payment, and also sign checks
    C. reconcile the bank statements, and also receive and deposit cash
    D. sign checks, and also cancel supporting documents

17. An internal accounting control questionnaire indicates that an approved receiving report is required to accompany every check request for payment of merchandise. 17.____
    Which of the following procedures provides the GREATEST assurance that this control is operating effectively?
    Select and examine

    A. cancelled checks and ascertain that the related receiving reports are dated no earlier than the checks
    B. cancelled checks and ascertain that the related receiving reports are dated no later than the checks
    C. receiving reports and ascertain that the related cancelled checks are dated no earlier than the receiving reports
    D. receiving reports and ascertain that the related cancelled checks are dated no later than the receiving reports

18. The completeness of EDP-generated sales figures can be tested by comparing the number of items listed on the daily sales report with the number of items billed on the actual invoices. 18.____
    This process uses

    A. check digits
    B. control totals
    C. validity tests
    D. process tracing data

19. For effective internal accounting control, employees maintaining the accounts receivable subsidiary ledger should NOT also approve 19.____

    A. employee overtime wages
    B. credit granted to customers
    C. write-offs of customer accounts
    D. cash disbursements

20. Based on a study and evaluation completed at an interim date, the auditor concludes that no significant internal accounting control weaknesses exist.
The records and procedures would MOST likely be tested again at year-end if 20.____

A. compliance tests were not performed by the internal auditor during the remaining period
B. the internal accounting control system provides a basis for reliance in reducing the extent of substantive testing
C. the auditor used nonstatistical sampling during the interim period compliance testing
D. inquiries and observations lead the auditor to believe that conditions have changed

21. After completing the preliminary phase of the review of internal accounting control, the auditor decides not to rely on the system to restrict substantive tests. Documentation may be limited to the auditor's 21.____

A. understanding of the internal accounting control system
B. reasons for deciding not to extend the review
C. basis for concluding that errors and irregularities will be prevented
D. completed internal accounting control questionnaire

Question 22.

DIRECTIONS: Question 22 is to be answered on the basis of the following diagram, which depicts the auditor's estimated deviation rate compared with the tolerable rate, and also depicts the true population deviation rate compared with the tolerable rate.

Auditor's Estimate Based on Sample Results	True State of Population: Deviation Rate Exceeds Tolerable Rate	True State of Population: Deviation Rate is Less Than Tolerable Rate
Deviation Rate Exceeds Tolerable Rate	I.	III.
Deviation Rate is Less Than Tolerable Rate	II.	IV.

22. As a result of compliance testing, the auditor underrelies on internal accounting control and thereby increases substantive testing.
This is illustrated by situation 22.____

A. I B. II C. III D. IV

23. Which of the following MOST likely constitutes a weakness in the internal accounting control of an EDP system?
The 23.____

A. control clerk establishes control over data received by the EDP department and reconciles control totals after processing
B. application programmer identifies programs required by the systems design and flowcharts the logic of these programs

C. systems analyst reviews output and controls the distribution of output from the EDP department
D. accounts payable clerk prepares data for computer processing and enters the data into the computer

24. Which of the following is LEAST likely to be evidence the auditor examines to determine whether operations are in compliance with the internal accounting control system? 24.____

A. Records documenting usage of EDP programs
B. Cancelled supporting documents
C. Confirmations of accounts receivable
D. Signatures on authorization forms

25. The PRIMARY purpose of a management advisory services engagement is to help the client 25.____

A. become more profitable by relying upon the CPA's existing personal knowledge about the client's business
B. improve the use of its capabilities and resources to achieve its objectives
C. document and quantify its future plans without impairing the CPA's objectivity or allowing the CPA to assume the role of management
D. obtain benefits that are guaranteed implicitly by the CPA

26. When unable to obtain sufficient competent evidential matter to determine whether certain client acts are illegal, the auditor would MOST likely issue 26.____

A. an unqualified opinion with a separate explanatory paragraph
B. either a qualified opinion or an adverse opinion
C. either a disclaimer or opinion or a qualified opinion,
D. either an adverse opinion or a disclaimer of opinion

27. Which of the following statements BEST describes the auditor's responsibility regarding the detection of material errors and irregularities? 27.____

A. The auditor is responsible for the failure to detect material errors and irregularities only when such failure results from the nonapplication of generally accepted accounting principles.
B. Extended auditing procedures are required to detect material errors and irregularities if the auditor's examination indicates that they may exist.
C. The auditor is responsible for the failure to detect material errors and irregularities only when the auditor fails to confirm receivables or observe inventories.
D. Extended auditing procedures are required to detect unrecorded transactions even if there is no evidence that material errors and irregularities may exist.

28. An abnormal fluctuation in gross profit that might suggest the need for extended audit procedures for sales and inventories would MOST likely be identified in the planning phase of the audit by the use of 28.____

A. tests of transactions and balances
B. a preliminary review of internal accounting control
C. specialized audit programs
D. analytical review procedures

29. When considering internal control, an auditor should be aware of the concept of reasonable assurance, which recognizes that the 29.____

    A. segregation of incompatible functions is necessary to ascertain that internal control is effective
    B. employment of competent personnel provides assurance that the objectives of internal control will be achieved
    C. establishment and maintenance of a system of internal control is an important responsibility of the management and not of the auditor
    D. cost of internal control should not exceed the benefits expected to be derived from internal control

30. When performing an audit of a city that is subject to the requirements of the Uniform Single Audit Act of 1984, an auditor should adhere to 30.____

    A. Governmental Accounting Standards Board GENERAL STANDARDS
    B. Governmental Finance Officers Association GOVERNMENTAL ACCOUNTING, AUDITING, AND FINANCIAL REPORTING PRINCIPLES
    C. General Accounting Office STANDARDS FOR AUDIT OF GOVERNMENTAL ORGANIZATIONS, PROGRAMS, ACTIVITIES, AND FUNCTIONS
    D. Securities and Exchange Commission REGULATION S-X

KEY (CORRECT ANSWERS)

1. D
2. B
3. A
4. C
5. D
6. C
7. B
8. D
9. D
10. D
11. C
12. C
13. C
14. B
15. A
16. D
17. B
18. B
19. C
20. D
21. B
22. C
23. C
24. C
25. B
26. C
27. B
28. D
29. D
30. C

EXAMINATION SECTION

TEST 1

DIRECTIONS: Select the best answer for each of the following items relating to a variety of not-for-profit and governmental accounting problems.

1. Payne Hospital received an unrestricted bequest of $100,000 in 2017. This bequest should be recorded as 1.______
   A. A memorandum entry only.
   B. Other operating revenue of $100,000.
   C. Nonoperating revenue of $100,000.
   D. A direct credit of $100,000 to the fund balance.

2. The following funds are among those maintained by Arlon City: 2.______

Enterprise funds	$2,000,000
Internal service funds	800,000

   Arlon's proprietary funds amount to
   A. $0
   B. $ 800,000
   C. $2,000,000
   D. $2,800,000

Items 3 and 4 are based on the following information pertaining to the sale of equipment by Nous Foundation, a voluntary health and welfare organization:

Sales price	$12,000
Cost	14,000
Carrying amount	10,000

Nous made the correct entry to record the $2,000 gain on sale.

3. The amount that should be debited and credited for the additional entry in connection with this sale is 3.______
   A. $ 2,000
   B. $10,000
   C. $12,000
   D. $14,000

4. The additional entry that Nous should record in connection with this sale is 4.______

	Debit	Credit
A.	Fund balance -- expended	Fund balance – unexpended
B.	Fund balance -- unexpended	Fund balance – expended
C.	Excess revenues control	Sale of equipment
D.	Current unrestricted funds	Fund balance – undesignated

5. Dodd Village received a gift of a new fire engine from a local resident. The fair market value of this fire engine was $200,000. The entry to be made in the general fixed assets account group for this gift is 5.______

		Debit	*Credit*
A.	Machinery and equipment	$200,000	
	Investment in general fixed assets from private gifts		$200,000
B.	Investment in general fixed assets	$200,000	
	Gift revenue		$200,000
C.	General fund assets	$200,000	
	Private gifts		$200,000
D.	Memorandum entry only	___	___

6. Burr City has approved a special assessment project providing for total assessments of $300,000, to be collected from affected property owners in five equal annual installments starting in 2018. The entry to be made to record the levy of assessments in 2018 is 6.______

		Debit	*Credit*
A.	Special assessments receivable ---- current	$ 60,000	
	Special assessments receivable ---- deferred	240,000	
	Revenues control		$ 60,000
	Deferred revenues		240,000
B.	Special assessments receivable ---- current	$ 60,000	
	Revenues control		$ 60,000
C.	Special assessments receivable	$300,000	
	Revenues control		$300,000
D.	Special assessments receivable	$300,000	
	Deferred revenues		$300,000

7. Lake City operates a centralized data processing center through an internal service fund, to provide data processing services to Lake's other governmental units. In 2001, this internal service fund billed Lake's water and sewer fund $100,000 for data processing services. How should the internal service fund record this billing?

7.______

	Debit	*Credit*
A. Memorandum entry only	----	----
B. Due from water and sewer fund	$100,000	
Data processing department expenses		$100,000
C. Intergovernmental transfers	$100,000	
Interfund exchanges		$100,000
D. Due from water and sewer fund	$100,000	
Operating revenues control		$100,000

8. Wells Township issued the following long-term obligations:

8.______

Revenue bonds to be repaid from admission fees collected by the township swimming pool	$500,000
General obligation bonds issued for the township water and sewer fund which will service the debt	900,000

Although the above-mentioned bonds are expected to be paid from enterprise funds, the full faith and credit of Wells Township has been pledged as further assurance that the liabilities will be paid. What amount of these bonds should be accounted for in the general long-term debt account group?

A. $1,400,000
B. $ 900,000
C. $ 500,000
D. $0

9. The following proceeds were received by Kew City from specific revenue sources that are legally restricted to expenditure for specified purposes:

9.______

Gasoline taxes to finance road repairs	$400,000
Levies on affected property owners to finance sidewalk repairs	300,000

The amount that should be accounted for in Kew's special revenue funds is

A. $0
B. $300,000
C. $400,000
D. $700,000

10. In 2017, Pyle Hospital received a $250,000 pure endowment fund grant. Also in 2017, Pyle's governing board designated, for special uses, $300,000 which had originated from unrestricted gifts. What amount of these resources should be accounted for as part of general (unrestricted) funds?
    A. $0
    B. $250,000
    C. $300,000
    D. $550,000

10.______

11. During 2017, Shaw Hospital purchased medicines for hospital use totaling $800,000. Included in this $800,000 was an invoice of $10,000 that was canceled in 2017 by the vendor because the vendor wished to donate this medicine to Shaw. This donation of medicine should be recorded as:
    A. A $10,000 reduction of medicine expense.
    B. An increase in other operating revenue of $10,000.
    C. A direct $10,000 credit to the general (unrestricted) funds balance.
    D. A $10,000 credit to the restricted funds balance.

11.______

12. Aviary Haven, a voluntary welfare organization funded by contributions from the general public, received unrestricted pledges of $500,000 during 2017. It was estimated that 12% of these pledges would be uncollectible. By the end of 2017, $400,000 of the pledges had been collected, and it was expected that $40,000 more would be collected in 2018, with the balance of $60,000 to be written of as uncollectible. Donors did **not** specify any periods during which the donations were to be used. What amount should Aviary include under public support in 2017 for net contributions?
    A. $500,000
    B. $452,000
    C. $440,000
    D. $400,000

12.______

13. In 2003, Menton City received $5,000,000 of bond proceeds to be used for capital projects. Of this amount, $1,000,000 was expended in 2018. Expenditures for the $4,000,000 balance were expected to be incurred in 2019. These bond proceeds should be recorded in capital projects funds for
    A. $5,000,000 in 2018.
    B. $5,000,000 in 2019.
    C. $1,000,000 in 2018 and $4,000,000 in 2019.
    D. $1,000,000 in 2018 and in the general fund for $4,000,000 in 2018.

13.______

14. The following information pertains to Wood Township's long-term debt: 14.______

Cash accumulations to cover payment of principal and interest on

General long-term obligations	$350,000
Proprietary fund obligations	$100,000

How much of these cash accumulations should be accounted for in Wood's debt service funds

A. 40 B. $100,000 C. $350,000 D. $450,000

15. Palma Hospital's patient service revenues for services provided in 2018, at established rates, amounted to $8,000,000 on the accrual basis. For internal reporting, Palma uses the discharge method. Under this method, patient service revenues are recognized only when patients are discharged, with no recognition given to revenues accruing for services to patients not yet discharged. Patient service revenues at established rates using the discharge method amounted to $7,000,000 for 2018. According to generally accepted accounting principles, Palma should report patient service revenues for 2018 of 15.______

A. Either $8,000,000 or $7,000,000, at the option of the hospital.
B. $8,000,000
C. $7,500,000
D. $7,000,000

16. The following receipts were among those recorded by Kerry College during 2018: 16.______

Unrestricted gifts	$500,000
Restricted current funds (expended for current operating purposes)	200,000
Restricted current funds (not yet expended)	100,000

The amount that should be included in current funds revenues is

A. $800,000
B. $700,000
C. $600,000
D. $500,000

17. Abbey University's unrestricted current funds comprised the following: 17.______

Assets	$5,000,000
Liabilities (including deferred revenues of $100,000)	3,000,000

The fund balance of Abbey's unrestricted current funds was

A. $1,900,000
B. $2,000,000
C. $2,100,000
D. $5,000,000

18. Park College is sponsored by a religious group. Volunteers from this religious group regularly contribute their services to Park, and are paid nominal amounts to cover their commuting costs. During 2018, the total amount paid to these volunteers aggregated $12,000. The gross value of services performed by them, determined by reference to lay-equivalent salaries, amounted to $300,000. What amount should Park record as expenditures in 2018 for these volunteers' services? 18.______
   A. $312,000
   B. $300,000
   C. $ 12,000
   D. $0

19. For the summer session of 2018, Ariba University assessed its students $1,700,000 (net of refunds), covering tuition and fees for educational and general purposes. However, only $1,500,000 was expected to be realized because scholarships totaling $150,000 were granted to students, and tuition remissions of $50,000 were allowed to faculty members' children attending Ariba. What amount should Ariba include in the unrestricted current funds as revenues from student tuition and fees? 19.______
   A. $1,500,000
   B. $1,550,000
   C. $1,650,000
   D. $1,700,000

20. Cura Hospital's property, plant, and equipment, net of depreciation, amounted to $10,000,000, with related mortgage liabilities of $1,000,000. What amount should be included in the restricted fund grouping? 20.______
   A. $0
   B. $ 1,000,000
   C. $ 9,000,000
   D. $10,000,000

21. Sara Loy is a member of a four-person equal partnership. In 2018, Sara sold 100 shares of a listed stock to the partnership for the stock's fair market value of $20,000. Sara's basis for this stock, that was purchased in 2011, was $14,000. Sara's recognized gain on the sale of this stock was 21.______
   A. $0
   B. $1,500
   C. $4,500
   D. $6,000

Items 22 and 23 are based on the following data:

Mike Reed, a partner in Post Co., received the following distribution from Post:

	Post's basis	*Fair market value*
Cash	$11,000	$11,000
Land	5,000	12,500

Before this distribution, Reed's basis in Post was $25,000.

22. If this distribution were in complete liquidation of Reed's interest in Post, Reed's basis for the land would be 22.______
A. $14,000
B. $12,500
C. $ 5,000
D. $ 1,500

23. If this distribution were nonliquidating, Reed's recognized gain or loss on the distribution would be 23.______
A. $11,000 gain.
B. $ 9,000 loss.
C. $ 1,500 loss.
D. $0.

24. Dave Cole's adjusted basis for his interest in Marb Associates, a partnership, was $50,000. This amount includes $20,000 of partnership liabilities for which Cole was personally liable. Marb had no unrealized receivables or substantially appreciated inventory. After having been paid his share of partnership income for the tax year, Cole sold his entire interest in Marb for $40,000 cash and a release from all partnership liabilities. Cole's recognized gain or loss on the sale of his interest in Marb was 24.______
A. $0.
B. $10,000 ordinary income.
C. $10,000 capital gain.
D. $10,000 capital loss.

25. Pursuant to a plan of corporate reorganization adopted in June 2018, Lois Pell exchanged 100 shares of Ral Corp. common stock that she had purchased in March 2018 at a cost of $10,000 for 150 shares of Lars Corp. common stock having a fair market value of $12,000. Pell's recognized gain on this exchange was 25.______
   A. $0.
   B. $2,000 ordinary income.
   C. $2,000 short-term capital gain.
   D. $2,000 long-term capital gain.

26. The accumulated earnings tax 26.______
   A. Should be self-assessed by filing a separate schedule along with the regular tax return.
   B. Applies only to closely held corporations.
   C. Can be imposed on S corporations that do not regularly distribute their earnings.
   D. Can **not** be imposed on a corporation that has undistributed earnings and profits of less than $150,000.

27. The personal holding company tax may be imposed 27.______
   A. As an alternative tax in place of the corporation's regularly computed tax.
   B. If more than 50% of the corporation's stock is owned, directly or indirectly, by more than ten stockholders.
   C. If at least 60% of the corporation's adjusted ordinary gross income for the taxable year is personal holding company income, and the stock ownership test is satisfied.
   D. In conjunction with the accumulated earnings tax.

28. To qualify as an exempt organization, the applicant 28.______
   A. Must fall into one of the specific classes upon which exemption is conferred by the Internal Revenue Code.
   B. Can **not**, under any circumstances, be a foreign corporation.
   C. Can **not**, under any circumstances, engage in lobbying activities.
   D. Can **not** be exclusively a social club.

29. Which one of the following statements is correct with regard to exempt organizations? 29.______
   A. An organization is automatically exempt from tax merely by meeting the statutory requirements for exemption.
   B. Exempt organizations that are required to file annual information returns must disclose the identity of all substantial contributors, in addition to the amount of contributions received.
   C. An organization will automatically forfeit its exempt status if any executive or other employee of the organization is paid compensation in excess of $150,000 per year, even if such compensation is reasonable.
   D. Exempt status of an organization may **not** be retroactively revoked.

30. If an exempt organization is a charitable trust, then unrelated business income is 30.______
    A. Not subject to tax.
    B. Taxed at rates applicable to corporations.
    C. Subject to tax even if such income is less than $1,000.
    D. Subject to tax only for the amount of such income in excess of $1,000.

KEY (CORRECT ANSWERS)

1. C	11. B	21. D
2. D	12. C	22. A
3. B	13. A	23. D
4. A	14. C	24. C
5. A	15. B	25. A
6. A	16. B	26. D
7. D	17. B	27. C
8. D	18. B	28. A
9. C	19. D	29. B
10. C	20. A	30. D

TEST 2

DIRECTIONS: Select the best answer for each of the following items relating to a variety of not-for-profit and governmental accounting problems.

1. If a corporation's tentative minimum tax exceeds the regular tax, the excess amount is   1.______
   A. Carried back to the preceding taxable year.
   B. Carried back to the third preceding taxable year.
   C. Payable in addition to the regular tax.
   D. Subtracted from the regular tax.

2. In the filing of a consolidated income tax return for a corporation and its wholly-owned subsidiaries, intercompany dividends between the parent and subsidiary corporations are   2.______
   A. Fully taxable.
   B. Included in taxable income to the extent of 80%.
   C. Included in taxable income to the extent of 20%.
   D. Not taxable.

3. For the year ended December 31, 2018, Bard Corp.'s income per accounting records, before federal income taxes, was $450,000 and included the following: 3.______

State corporate income tax refunds	$ 4,000
Life insurance proceeds on officer's death	15,000
Net loss on sale of securities bought for investment in 2007	20,000

   Bard's 2018 taxable income was
   A. $435,000
   B. $451,000
   C. $455,000
   D. $470,000

4. Tau Corp., which has been operating since 2011, has an October 31 year end, which coincides with its natural business year. On May 15, 2018, Tau filed the required form to elect S corporation status. All of Tau's stockholders consented to the election, and all other requirements were met. The earliest date that Tau can be recognized as an S corporation is   4.______
   A. November 1, 2017.
   B. May 15, 2018.
   C. November 1, 2018.
   D. November 1, 2019.

Items 5 through 10 are based on the following data:

Eric Bay was the sole stockholder of Lee Corp., an accrual basis taxpayer engaged principally in retailing operations. Lee's retained earnings at December 31, 2017, amounted to $2,000,000. For the year ended December 31, 2018, Lee's book income, before income taxes, was $600,000. Included in the computation of this $600,000 were the following:

Gain on sale of land used in business	$ 20,000
Loss on sale of long-term investments in marketable securities	30,000
Dividend income from unaffiliated taxable domestic corporations	4,000
Keyman insurance premiums paid on Bay's life (Lee is beneficiary)	1,000
Group term life insurance premiums paid on $25,000 life insurance policies for employees (employees' dependents are beneficiaries)	15,000
Contribution to State University (authorized by Board of Directors in December 2018; to be paid March 3, 2019)	100,000
Amortization of organization costs (total organization costs of $6,000 were incurred in January 2015, and are being amortized over a 10-year period for financial statement purposes)	600

In 2011, Lee had reacquired 1,000 shares of its own $10 par common stock at a cost of $25,000. This stock was held as treasury stock until May 2018, when it was reissued to James Smith at its fair market value of $33,000.

5. How much should Lee report in its 2018 return as long-term capital gain on the issuance of its treasury stock to Smith? 5.______
   A. $0
   B. $ 8,000
   C. $23,000
   D. $33,000

6. In computing taxable income for 2018, what is the maximum deduction that Lee can claim for organization costs, assuming that the appropriate election was made on a timely basis? 6.______
   A. $1,200
   B. $ 600
   C. $ 300
   D. $0

7. With regard to Lee's contribution to State University, Lee can 7.______
   A. Not deduct any portion of the $100,000 in 2018, because the contribution was not paid until 2019.
   B. Deduct the entire $100,000 in its 2018 return.
   C. Elect to carry back to 2017 a portion of the $100,000 that does not exceed the deduction ceiling for 2017 and 2018.
   D. Elect to deduct in its 2018 return any portion of the $100,000 that does not exceed the deduction ceiling for 2018.

8. In computing taxable income for 2018, what amount should Lee deduct for keyman and group life insurance premiums? 8.______
   A. $ 8,000
   B. $15,000
   C. $15,500
   D. $16,000

9. The dividend income Lee should include in its 2018 taxable income is 9.______
   A. $4,000
   B. $3,200
   C. $ 800
   D. $0

10. In computing taxable income for 2018, Lee should deduct a net capital loss of 10.______
   A. $15,000
   B. $10,000
   C. $ 5,000
   D. $0

Items 11 through 13 are based on the following data:

In 2010, Iris King bought a diamond necklace for her own use, at a cost of $10,000. In 2017, when the fair market value was $12,000, Iris gave this necklace to her daughter, Ruth. No gift tax was due.

11. If Ruth sells this diamond necklace in 2018 for $13,000, Ruth's recognized gain would be 11.______
   A. $3,000
   B. $2,000
   C. $1,000
   D. $0

12. This diamond necklace is a 12.______
    A. Capital asset.
    B. Section 1231 asset.
    C. Section 1245 asset.
    D. Section 1250 asset.

13. Ruth's holding period for this gift 13.______
    A. Starts in 2018.
    B. Starts in 2011.
    C. Depends on whether the necklace is sold by Ruth at a gain or at a loss.
    D. Is irrelevant because Ruth received the necklace for no consideration of money or money's worth.

14. In 2018, Sam Dunn provided more than half the support for his wife, his father's brother, and his cousin. Sam's wife was the only relative who was a member of Sam's household. None of the relatives had any income, nor did any of them file an individual or a joint return. All of these relatives are U.S. citizens. Which of these relatives should be claimed as a dependent or dependents on Sam's 2018 return? 14.______
    A. Only his wife.
    B. Only his father's brother.
    C. Only his cousin.
    D. His wife, his father's brother, and his cousin.

15. Ben Carr, a calendar-year taxpayer, was 65 years old on December 30, 2017. Ben filed his 2017 individual income tax return on April 1, 2018, and attached a check for the balance of tax due as shown on the return. On August 15, 2018, Ben realized that he had inadvertently failed to claim the additional exemption to which he was entitled by virtue of having attained age 65 in 2017. In order for Ben to recover the tax that he would have saved by claiming the extra exemption, he must file a refund claim no later than 15.______
    A. December 31, 2018.
    B. April 1, 2021.
    C. April 15, 2021.
    D. August 15, 2021.

16. If a taxpayer omits from his or her income tax return an amount that exceeds 25% of the gross income reported on the return, the Internal Revenue Service can issue a notice of deficiency within a maximum period of 16.______
    A. 3 years from the date the return was filed, if filed before the due date.
    B. 3 years from the date the return was due, if filed by the due date.
    C. 6 years from the date the return was filed, if filed before the due date.
    D. 6 years from the date the return was due, if filed by the due date.

17. Smith and Jones, both U.S. citizens, died in 2018. Neither made any lifetime gifts. At the dates of death, Smith's gross estate was $510,000, and Jones' gross estate was $610,000. A federal estate tax return must be filed for 17.______

	Smith	*Jones*
A.	Yes	Yes
B.	No	No
C.	Yes	No
D.	No	Yes

Items 18 through 20 are based on the following data:

Alan Curtis, a U.S. citizen, died on March 1, 2018, leaving an adjusted gross estate with a fair market value of $1,400,000 at the date of death. Under the terms of Alan's will, $375,000 was bequeathed outright to his widow, free of all estate and inheritance taxes. The remainder of Alan's estate was left to his mother. Alan made no taxable gifts during his lifetime.

18. If the executor of Alan's estate elects the alternate valuation method, all remaining undistributed property included in the gross estate must be valued as of how many months after Alan's death? 18.______
    A. 12
    B. 9
    C. 6
    D. 3

19. In computing the taxable estate, the executor of Alan's estate should claim a marital deduction of 19.______
    A. $ 250,000
    B. $ 375,000
    C. $ 700,000
    D. $1,025,000

20. Disregarding extensions of time for filing, within how many months after the date of Alan's death is the federal estate tax return due? 20.______
    A. $2\frac{1}{2}$
    B. $3\frac{1}{2}$
    C. 9
    D. 12

21. Paul Crane, age 25, and single with no dependents, had an adjusted gross income of $30,000 in 2018, exclusive of $2,000 in unemployment compensation benefits received in 2018. The amount of Crane's unemployment compensation benefits taxable for 2018 is
    A. $2,000
    B. $1,000
    C. $ 500
    D. $0

21.______

22. In 2018, Gail Judd received the following dividends from

22.______

Benefit Life Insurance Co., on Gail's life insurance policy (Total dividends received have not yet exceeded accumulated premiums paid)	$100
Safe National Bank, on bank's common stock	300
Roe Mfg. Corp., a Delaware corporation, on preferred stock	500

What amount of dividend income should Gail report in her 2018 income tax return?
    A. $900
    B. $800
    C. $500
    D. $300

23. Under a $150,000 insurance policy on her deceased father's life, Mary Green is to receive $12,000 per year for 15 years. Of the $12,000 received in 2018, the amount subject to income tax is
    A. $0
    B. $ 1,000
    C. $ 2,000
    D. $12,000

23.______

24. The following information pertains to installment sales of personal use property made by Fred Dale in his retail furniture store:

24.______

Year of sale	*Installment sales*	*Gross profit*	*Collections in 2002*
2016	$ 50,000	$15,000	$10,000
2017	100,000	40,000	30,000
2018	150,000	75,000	40,000

These sales were **not** under a revolving credit plan. Under the installment method, Dale should report gross profit for 2018 of
A. $ 35,000
B. $ 75,000
C. $ 80,000
D. $130,000

25. Under the cash method of reporting, an individual should report gross income 25.______
A. Only for the year in which income is actually received n cash.
B. Only for the year in which income is actually received either in cash or in property.
C. For the year in which income is either actually or constructively received n cash only.
D. For the year in which income is either actually or constructively received either in cash or in property.

26. For the year ended December 31, 2017, Don Raff earned $1,000 interest at Ridge Savings Bank on a certificate of deposit scheduled to mature in 2019. In January 2018, before filing his 2017 income tax return, Raff incurred a forfeiture penalty of $500 for premature withdrawal of the funds. Raff should treat this $500 forfeiture penalty as a 26.______
A. Reduction of interest earned in 2017, so that only $500 of such interest is taxable on Raff's 2017 return.
B. Deduction from 2018 adjusted gross income, deductible only if Raff itemizes his deductions for 2018.
C. Penalty **not** deductible for tax purposes.
D. Deduction from gross income in arriving at 2018 adjusted gross income.

27. With regard to tax recognition of alimony in connection with a 2018 divorce, which one of the following statements is correct? 27.______
A. The divorced couple may be members of the same household at the time payments are made.
B. Payments may be made either in cash or in property.
C. If the payor spouse pays premiums for insurance on his life as a requirement under the divorce agreement, the premiums are alimony if the payor spouse owns the policy.
D. Payments must terminate at the death of the payee spouse.

28. Emil Gow owns a two-family house which has two identical apartments. Gow lives in one apartment and rents out the other. In 2018, the rental apartment was fully occupied and Gow received $7,200 in rent. During the year ended December 31,2018, Gow paid the following: 28.______

Real estate taxes	$6,400
Painting of rental apartment	800
Annual fire insurance premium	600

In 2018, depreciation for the entire house was determined to be $5,000. What amount should Gow include in his adjusted gross income for 2002?
A. $2,900
B. $ 800
C. $ 400
D. $ 100

29. In 2018, Al Oran bought a paved vacant lot adjacent to his retail store for use as a customers' parking lot at a cost of $15,000. In addition, Oran bought new store fixtures costing $8,000. What portion of these assets constitutes capital assets? 29.______
A. $0
B. $ 8,000
C. $15,000
D. $23,000

30. John Budd files a joint return with his wife. Budd's employer pays 100% of the cost of all employees' group-term life insurance under a qualified plan. Under this plan, the maximum amount of tax-free coverage that may be provided for Budd by his employer is 30.______
A. $100,000
B. $ 50,000
C. $ 10,000
D. $ 5,000

KEY (CORRECT ANSWERS)

1. C	11. A	21. A
2. D	12. A	22. B
3. C	13. B	23. C
4. C	14. B	24. A
5. A	15. C	25. D
6. A	16. D	26. D
7. D	17. D	27. D
8. B	18. C	28. C
9. C	19. B	29. A
10. D	20. C	30. B

INTERPRETING STATISTICAL DATA GRAPHS, CHARTS, AND TABLES

EXAMINATION SECTION

TEST 1

DIRECTIONS: Each question or incomplete statement is followed by several suggested answers or completions. Select the one that BEST answers the question or completes the statement. *PRINT THE LETTER OF THE CORRECT ANSWER IN THE SPACE AT THE RIGHT.*

Questions 1-5.

DIRECTIONS: Questions 1 through 5 are to be answered SOLELY on the basis of the following chart.

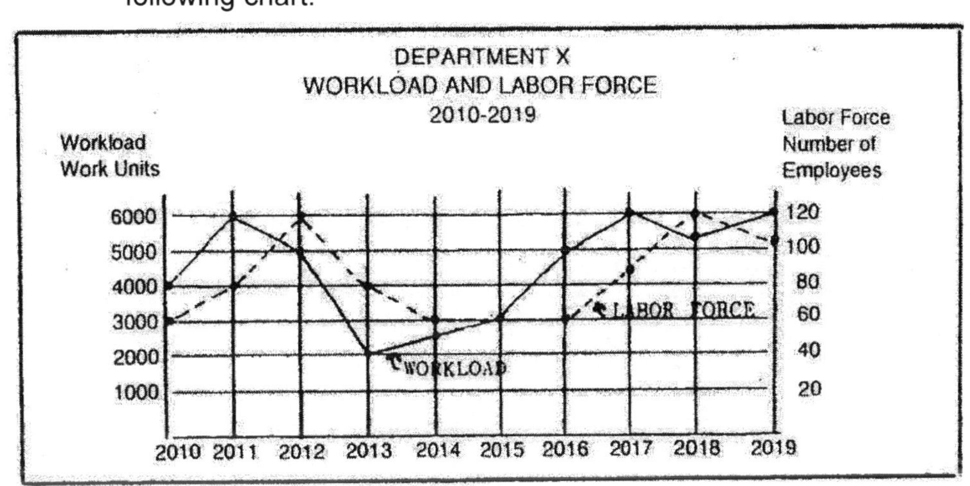

1. The one of the following years for which average employee production was LOWEST was 1.____
   A. 2011 B. 2013 C. 2015 D. 2017

2. The average annual employee production for the ten-year period was, in terms of work units, MOST NEARLY 2.
   A. 30 B. 50 C. 70 D. 80

3. On the basis of the chart, it can be deduced that personnel needs for the coming year are budgeted on the basis of 3.____
   A. workload for the current year
   B. expected workload for the coming year
   C. no set plan]
   D. average workload over the five years immediately preceding the period

4. The chart indicates that the operation is carefully programmed and that the labor force has been used properly. 4.____
   This opinion is
   A. *supported* by the chart; the organization has been able to meet emergency situations requiring more additional work without commensurate increases in staff
   B. *not supported* by the chart; the irregular workload shows a complete absence of planning
   C. *supported* by the chart; the similar shapes of the WORKLOAD and LABOR FORCE curves show that these important factors are closely related
   D. *not supported* by the chart; poor planning with respect to labor requirements is obvious from the chart

5. The chart indicates that the department may be organized in such a way as to require a permanent minimum staff which is too large for the type of operation indicated. 5.____
   This opinion is
   A. *supported* by the chart; there is no indication that the operation calls for an irreducible minimum number of employees and application of the most favorable work production records show this to be too high for normal operation
   B. *not supported* by the chart; the absence of any sort of regularity makes it impossible to express any opinion with any degree of certainty
   C. *supported* by the chart; the expected close relationship between workload and labor force is displaced somewhat, a phenomenon which usually occurs as a result of a fixed minimum requirement
   D. *not supported* by the chart; the violent movement of the LABOR FORCE curve makes it evident that no minimum requirements are in effect

---

KEY (CORRECT ANSWERS)

1. B
2. B
3. A
4. D
5. A

TEST 2

Questions 1-4.

DIRECTIONS: Questions 1 through 4 are to be answered SOLELY on the basis of the chart below, which shows the annual average number of administrative actions completed for the four divisions of a bureau. Assume that the figures remain stable from year to year.

	DIVISIONS				
Administrative Actions	W	X	Y	Z	TOTALS
Telephone Inquiries Answered	8,000	6,800	7,500	4,800	27,100
Interviews Conducted	500	630	550	500	2,180
Applications Processed	15,000	18,000	14,500	9,500	57,000
Letters Typed	2,500	4,400	4,350	3,250	14,500
Reports Completed	200	250	100	50	600
Totals	26,200	30,080	27,000	18,100	101,380

1. In which division is the number of Applications Processed the GREATEST percentage of the total Administrative Actions for that division? 1.____
   A. W   B.   C. Y   D. Z

2. The bureau chief is considering a plan that would consolidate the typing of letters in a separate unit. This unit would be responsible for the typing of letters for all divisions in which the number of letters typed exceeds 15% of the total number of administrative actions. 2.____
   Under this plan, which of the following divisions would CONTINUE to type its own letters?
   A. W and X   B. W, X, and Y   C. X and Y   D. X and Z

3. The setting up of a central information service that would be capable of answering 25% of the whole bureau's telephone inquiries is under consideration. Under such a plan, the divisions would gain for other activities that time previously spent on telephone inquiries. 3.____
   Approximately how much total time would such a service gain for all four divisions if it requires 5 minutes to answer the average telephone inquiry?
   ______ hours,
   A. 500   B. 515   C. 565   D. 585

4. Assume that the rate of production shown in the table can be projected as accurate for the coming year and that monthly output is constant for each type of administrative action within a division. Division Y is scheduled to work exclusively on a four-month long special project during that year. During the period of the project, Division Y's regular workload will be divided evenly among the remaining divisions. 4.____
   Using the figures in the table, what would be MOST NEARLY the percentage increase in the total Administrative Actions completed by Division Z for the year?
   A. 8%   B. 16%   C. 25%   D. 50%

KEY (CORRECT ANSWERS)

1. B
2. A
3. C
4. B

TEST 3

Questions 1-3.

DIRECTIONS: The management study of employee absence due to sickness is an effective tool in planning. Questions 1 through 3 are to be answered SOLELY on the basis of the data below.

Number of Days Absent Per Worker (Sickness)	1	2	3	4	5	6	7	8 OR OVER
Number of Workers	76	23	6	3	1	0	1	0
Total Number of Workers: 400								
Period Covered: Jan. 1 – Dec. 31								

1. The TOTAL number of man days lost due to illness was 1.____
   A. 110 B. 137 C. 144 D. 164

2. What percent of the workers had 4 or more days absence due to sickness? 2.____
   A. .25% B. 2.5% C. 1.25% D. 12.5%

3. Of the 400 workers studied, the number who lost no days due to sickness was 3.____
   A. 190 B. 236 C. 290 D. 346

KEY (CORRECT ANSWERS)

1. D
2. C
3. C

TEST 4

Questions 1-3.

DIRECTIONS: In the graph below, the lines labeled A and B represent the cumulative progress in the work of two file clerks, each of whom was given 500 consecutively numbered applications to file in the proper cabinets over a five-day work week. Questions 1 through 3 are to be answered SOLELY on the basis of the data provided in the graph.

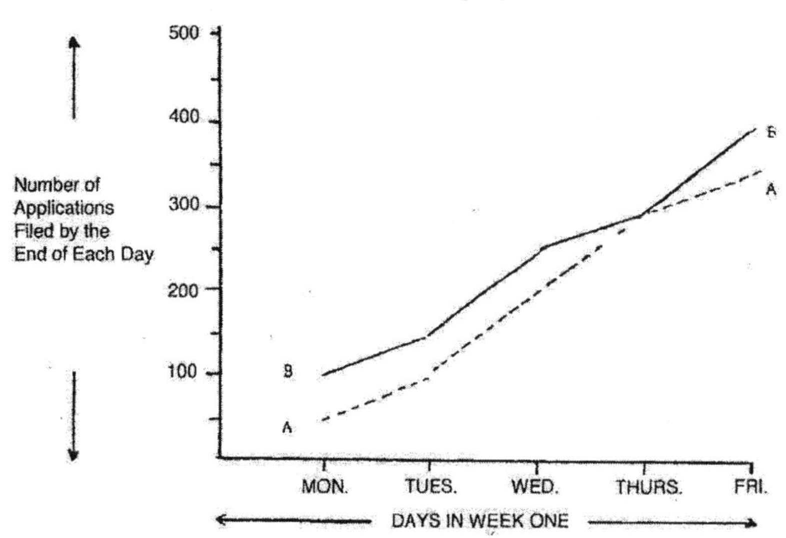

1. The day during which the LARGEST number of applications was filed by both clerks was
   A. Monday B. Tuesday C. Wednesday D. Friday

1.____

2. At the end of the second day, the percentage of applications still to be filed was
   A. 25% B. 50% C. 66% D. 75%

2.____

3. Assuming that the production pattern is the same the following week as the week shown in the chart, the day on which the file clerks will finish this assignment will be
   A. Monday B. Tuesday C. Wednesday D. Friday

3.____

KEY (CORRECT ANSWERS)

1. C
2. D
3. B

TEST 5

Questions 1-3.

DIRECTIONS: Questions 1 through 3 are to be answered SOLELY on the basis of the following information given in the following chart.

Number of Employees Producing Work-Units Within Range in 2009	Number of Work-Units Produced	Number of Employees Producing Work-Units Within Range in 2019
7	500-1000	4
14	1001-1500	11
26	1501-2000	28
22	2001-2500	36
17	2501-3000	39
10	3001-3500	23
4	3501-4000	9

1. Assuming that within each range of work-units produced, the average production was at the mid-point at that range (e.g., category 500-1000 = 750), then the AVERAGE number of work-units produced per employee in 2019 fell into the range 1.____
   A. 1001-1500 B. 1501-2000 C. 2001-2500 D. 2501-3000

2. The ratio of the number of employees producing more than 2000 work-units in 2009 to the number of employees producing more than 2000 work units in 2019 is MOST NEARLY 2.____
   A. 1:2 B. 2:3 C. 3:4 D. 4:5

3. In Department D, which of the following were GREATER in 2019 than in 2009? 3.____
   I. Total number of employees
   II. Total number of work-units produced
   III. Number of employees producing 2000 or fewer work-units
   The CORRECT answer is:
   A. I, II, and III B. I and II, but not III
   C. I and III, but not II D. II and III, but not I

KEY (CORRECT ANSWERS)

1. C
2. A
3. B

TEST 6

Questions 1-9.

DIRECTIONS: Questions 1 through 9 are to be answered SOLELY on the basis of the information contained in the following four charts which relate to a municipal department. These charts show for the fiscal year the total departmental expenditures for salaries for all its employees; the distribution of expenditures for salaries for permanent employees by title; the distribution of all employees, both permanent and temporary by title; and the distribution of temporary employees by title.

For Departmental Expenditures For Salaries For Fiscal Year.
Total: $129,000,000

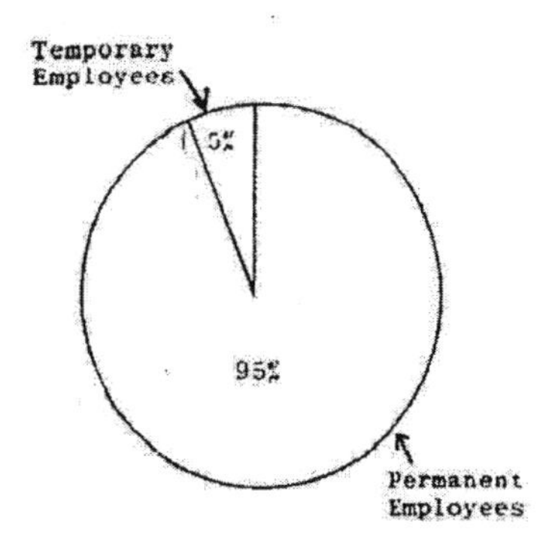

Distribution of Expenditures For Salaries For Permanent Employees, By Title.

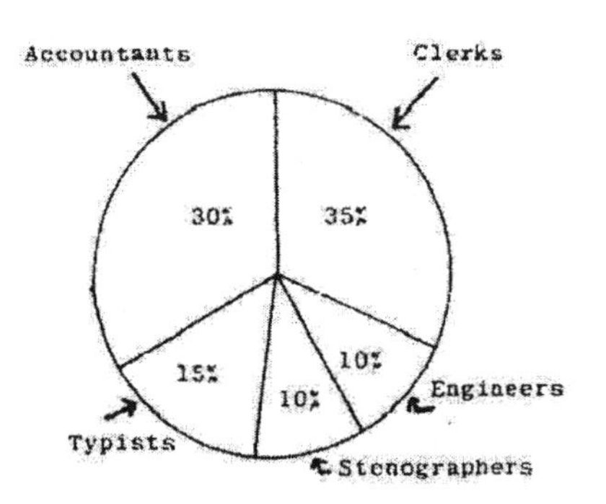

Distribution of All Employees, Both Permanent and Temporary, By Title.
Total Number of Employees: 3,200

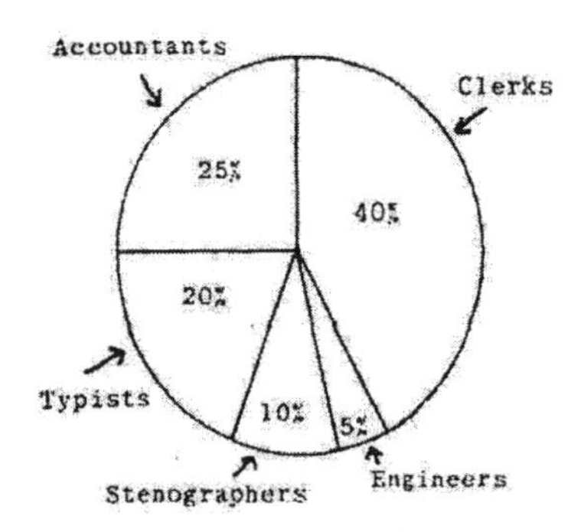

Distribution of Temporary Employees, By Title.
Total Number of Temporary Employees: 150

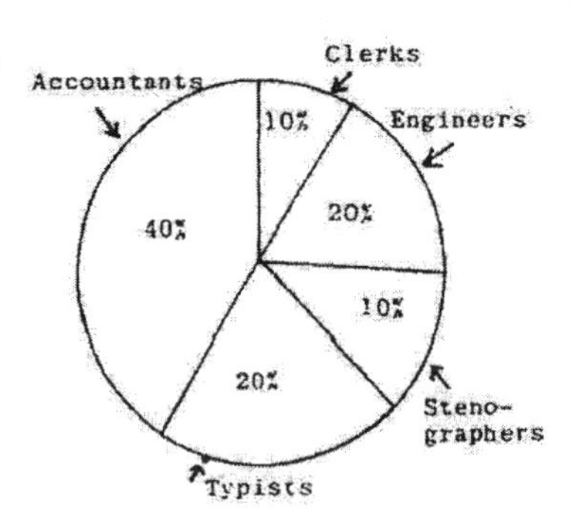

SAMPLE COMPUTATION

The total amount of money expended for the salaries of all the permanent typists can be computed as follows:

By taking 95% of $129,000,000, the total amount of money expended for the salaries of all permanent employees can be obtained. The total amount of money expended for the salaries of all the permanent typists can then be obtained by taking 15% of the money expended for the salaries of all permanent employees.

The answer is $18,382,500.

Candidates may find it useful to arrange their computations on their scratch paper in an orderly manner since the correct computations for one question may also be helpful in answering another question.

1. The TOTAL number of permanent typists is 1.____
   A. 640 B. 670 C. 608 D. 610

2. Of the total departmental expenditures for salaries for both permanent and temporary employees, the percentage allotted to permanent clerks is MOST NEARLY 2.____
   A. 25% B. 31% C. 33% D. 35%

3. The number of permanent employees who are NOT engineers is 3.____
   A. 2,890 B. 3,070 C. 3,040 D. 2,920

4. Assume that the average annual salary of the temporary accountants is $40000. Then, the average annual salary of the permanent accountants exceeds the average annual salary of the temporary accountants by MOST NEARLY 4.____
   A. 25% B. 20% C. 75% D. 40%

5. The average annual salary of the permanent clerks is MOST NEARLY 5.____
   A. $33,300 B. $33,900 C. $35,250 D. $35,700

6. If the temporary stenographers receive 8% of the total salaries allotted to temporary employees, then the average annual salary of the temporary stenographers is MOST NEARLY 6.____
   A. $34,500 B. $38,500 C. $36,000 D. $40,000

7. Assume that the temporary typists receive an average annual salary that is 3% less than the average annual salary that is paid to the permanent typists. Then, the average annual salary of the temporary typists is MOST NEARLY 7.____
   A. $27,850 B. $29,250 C. $30,000 D. $32,150

8. Assume that the average annual salary of the permanent engineers exceeds the average annual salary of the temporary engineers by $30,000. Then, the percentage of the total departmental expenditures for salaries for temporary employees that is allotted to temporary engineers is MOST NEARLY 8.____
   A. 15% B. 20% C. 25% D. 30%

9. If one-half of the permanent accountants earn an average of $45,000 per annum, then the average annual salary of the other permanent accounts is MOST NEARLY 9.____
   A. $51,150 B. $51,750 C. $54,350 D. $57,100

KEY (CORRECT ANSWERS)

1.	D	6.	A
2.	C	7.	B
3.	D	8.	D
4.	A	9.	C
5.	B		

TEST 7

Questions 1-6.

DIRECTIONS: Questions 1 through 6 are to be answered SOLELY on the basis of the information contained in the five charts below.

NUMBER OF UNITS OF WORK PRODUCED IN THE BUREAU PER YEAR

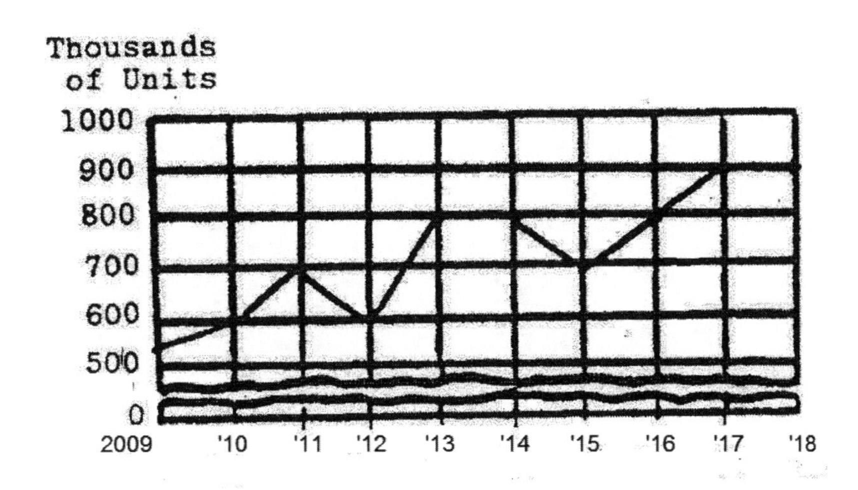

INCREASE IN THE NUMBER OF UNITS OF WORK PRODUCED IN 2018 OVER THE NUMBER PRODUCED IN 2009, BY BOROUGH

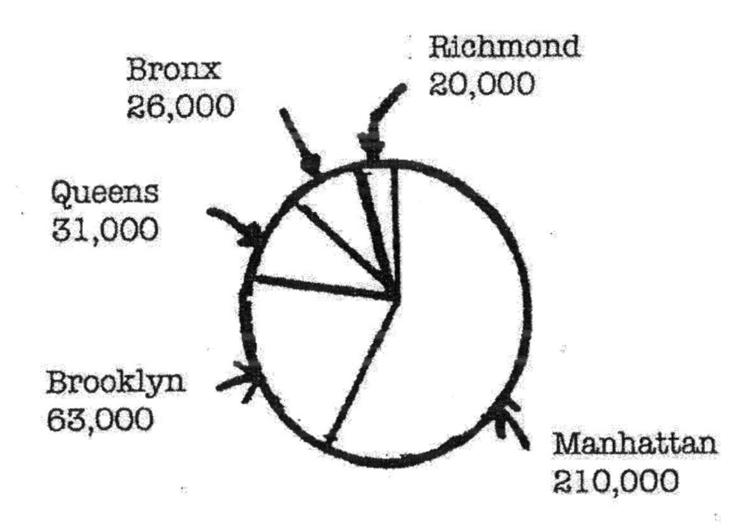

NUMBER OF MALE AND FEMALE EMPLOYEES PRODUCING THE UNITS OF WORK IN THE BUREAU PER YEAR

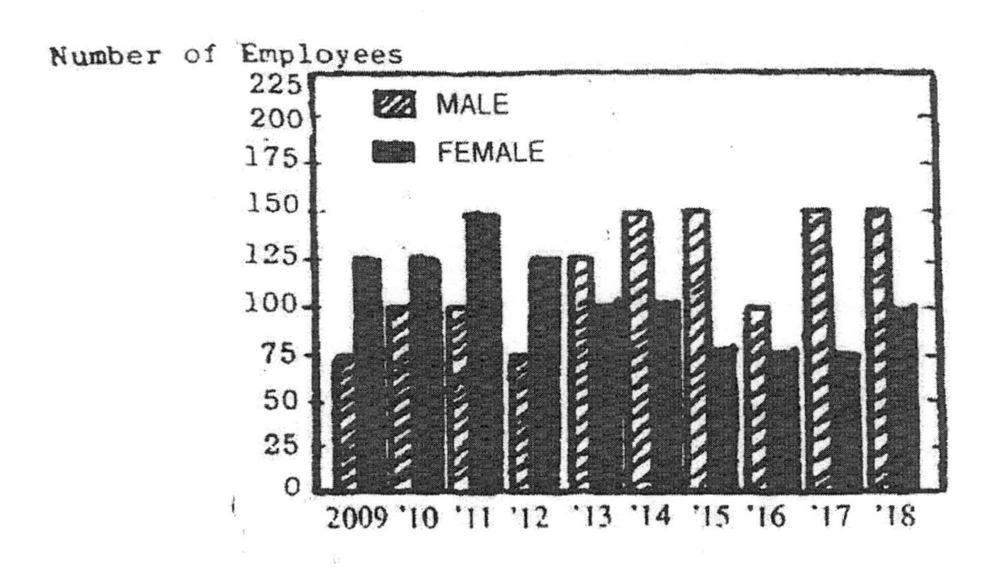

DISTRIBUTION OF THE AGES BY PERCENT OF EMPLOYEES ASSIGNED TO PRODUCE THE UNITS OF WORK IN THE YEARS 2009 AND 2018

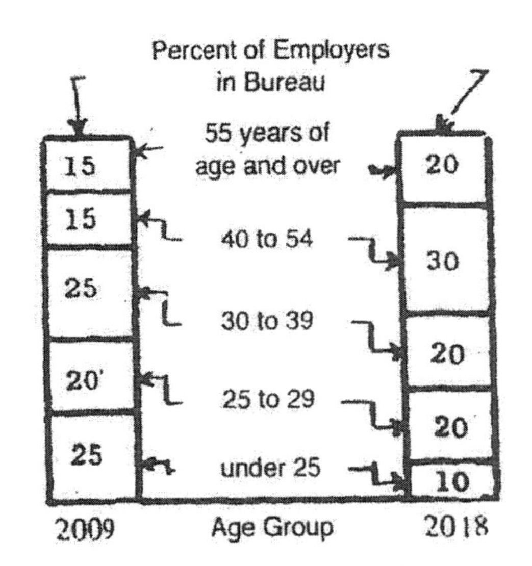

TOTAL SALARIES PAID PER YEAR TO EMPLOYEES ASSIGNED TO PRODUCE THE UNITS OF WORK IN THE BUREAU

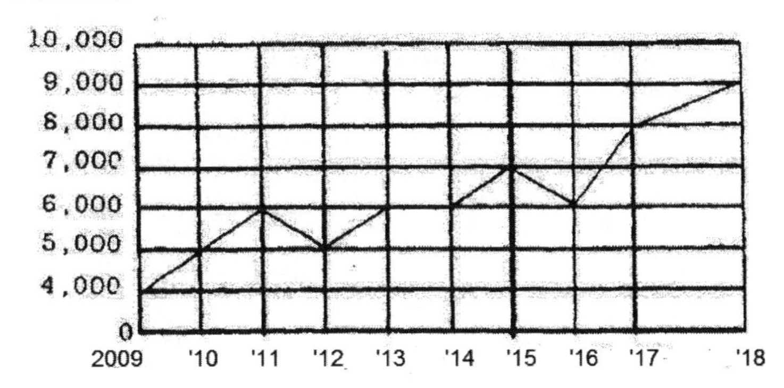

1. The information contained in the charts is sufficient to determine the 1.____
   A. amount of money paid in salaries to employees working in Richmond in 2018
   B. difference between the average annual salary of employees in the Bureau in 2018 and their average annual salary in 2017
   C. number of female employees in the Bureau between 30 and 39 years of age who were employed in 2009
   D. cost, in salary for the average male employee in the Bureau to produce 100 units of work in 2014

2. The one of the following which was GREATER, in the Bureau, in 2014 than it was in 2012 was the 2.____
   A. cost, in salaries, of producing a unit of work
   B. units of work produced annually per employee
   C. proportion of female employees to total number of employees
   D. average annual salary per employee

3. If, in 2018, one-half of the employees in the Bureau 55 years of age and over each earned an annual salary of $42,000, then the average annual salary of all the remaining employees in the Bureau was MOST NEARLY 3.____
   A. $31,750 B. $34,500 C. $35,300 D. $35,800

4. Assume that, in 2009, the offices in Richmond and the Bronx each produced the same number of units of work. Also assume that, in 2009, the offices in Brooklyn, Manhattan, and Queens each produced twice as many units of work as were produced in either of the other two boroughs. Then, the number of units of work produced in Brooklyn in 2008 was MOST NEARLY 4.____
   A. 69,000 B. 138,000 C. 201,000 D. 225,000

5. If, in 2016, the average annual salary of the female employees in the Bureau was four-fifths as large as the average annual salary of the male employees, then the average annual salary of the female employees in that year was   5.____
   A. $37,500   B. $31,000   C. $30,500   D. $30,000

6. Of the total number of employees in the Bureau who were 30 years of age and over in 2009, _____ must have been _____.   6.____
   A. at least 35; females
   B. less than 75; males
   C. no more than 100; females
   D. more than 15; males

KEY (CORRECT ANSWERS)

1. B
2. B
3. C
4. C
5. D
6. A

PREPARING WRITTEN MATERIAL

EXAMINATION SECTION

TEST 1

DIRECTIONS: Each of the sentences in this test may be classified under one of the following four categories:

A. *Incorrect* because of faulty grammar or sentence structure
B. *Incorrect* because of faulty punctuation
C. *Incorrect* because of faulty capitalization
D. *Correct*

Examine each sentence carefully to determine under which of the above four options it is best classified. Then, in the space at the right, print the capital letter preceding the option which is the BEST of the four suggested above.

(Each incorrect sentence contains but one type of error. Consider a sentence to be correct if it contains none of the types of errors mentioned, even though there may be other correct ways of expressing the same thought.)

1. This fact, together with those brought out at the previous meeting, prove that the schedule is satisfactory to the employees. 1.____

2. Like many employees in scientific fields, the work of bookkeepers and accountants requires accuracy and neatness. 2.____

3. "What can I do for you," the secretary asked as she motioned to the visitor to take a seat. 3.____

4. Our representative, Mr. Charles will call on you next week to determine whether or not your claim has merit. 4.____

5. We expect you to return in the spring; please do not disappoint us. 5.____

6. Any supervisor, who disregards the just complaints of his subordinates, is remiss in the performance of his duty. 6.____

7 Because she took less than an hour for lunch is no reason for permitting her to leave before five o'clock. 7.____

8. "Miss Smith," said the supervisor, "Please arrange a meeting of the staff for two o'clock on Monday." 8.____

9. A private company's vacation and sick leave allowance usually differs considerably from a public agency. 9.____

10. Therefore, in order to increase the efficiency of operations in the department, a report on the recommended changes in procedures was presented to the departmental committee in charge of the program. 10.____

11. We told him to assign the work to whoever was available. 11.____

12. Since John was the most efficient of any other employee in the bureau, he received the highest service rating. 12.____

13. Only those members of the national organization who resided in the middle West attended the conference in Chicago. 13.____

14. The question of whether the office manager has as yet attained, or indeed can ever hope to secure professional status is one which has been discussed for years. 14.____

15. No one knew who to blame for the error which, we later discovered, resulted in a considerable loss of time. 15.____

KEY (CORRECT ANSWERS)

1.	A	6.	B	11.	D
2.	A	7.	A	12.	A
3.	B	8.	C	13.	C
4.	B	9.	A	14.	B
5.	D	10.	D	15.	A

TEST 2

DIRECTIONS: Each of the sentences in this test may be classified under one of the following four categories:

A. *Incorrect* because of faulty grammar or sentence structure
B. *Incorrect* because of faulty punctuation
C. *Incorrect* because of faulty capitalization
D. *Correct*

1. The National alliance of Businessmen is trying to persuade private businesses to hire youth in the summertime. 1.____

2. The supervisor who is on vacation, is in charge of processing vouchers. 2.____

3. The activity of the committee at its conferences is always stimulating. 3.____

4. After checking the addresses again, the letters went to the mailroom. 4.____

5. The director, as well as the employees, are interested in sharing the dividends. 5.____

KEY (CORRECT ANSWERS)

1. C
2. B
3. D
4. A
5. A

TEST 3

DIRECTIONS: In each of the following groups of sentences, one of the four sentences is faulty in grammar, punctuation, or capitalization. Select the INCORRECT sentence in each case.

1. A. Sailing down the bay was a thrilling experience for me. 1.____
   B. He was not consulted about your joining the club.
   C. This story is different than the one I told you yesterday.
   D. There is no doubt about his being the best player.

2. A. He maintains there is but one road to world peace. 2.____
   B. It is common knowledge that a child sees much he is not supposed to see.
   C. Much of the bitterness might have been avoided if arbitration had been resorted to earlier in the meeting.
   D. The man decided it would be advisable to marry a girl somewhat younger than him.

3. A. In this book, the incident I liked least is where the hero tries to put out the forest fire. 3.____
   B. Learning a foreign language will undoubtedly give a person a better understanding of his mother tongue.
   C. His actions made us wonder what he planned to do next.
   D. Because of the war, we were unable to travel during the summer vacation.

4. A. The class had no sooner become interested in the lesson than the dismissal bell rang. 4.____
   B. There is little agreement about the kind of world to be planned at the peace conference.
   C. "Today," said the teacher, "we shall read 'The Wind in the Willows,' I am sure you'll like it.
   D. The terms of the legal settlement of the family quarrel handicapped both sides for many years.

5. A. I was so surprised that I was not able to say a word. 5.____
   B. She is taller than any other member of the class.
   C. It would be much more preferable if you were never seen in his company.
   D. We had no choice but to excuse her for being late.

KEY (CORRECT ANSWERS)

1. C
2. D
3. A
4. C
5. C

TEST 4

DIRECTIONS: In each of the following groups of sentences, one of the four sentences is faulty in grammar, punctuation, or capitalization. Select the INCORRECT sentence in each case.

1. A. Please send me these data at the earliest opportunity.
   B. The loss of their material proved to be a severe handicap.
   C. My principal objection to this plan is that it is impracticable.
   D. The doll had laid in the rain for an hour and was ruined.

   1.____

2. A. The garden scissors, left out all night in the rain, were in a badly rusted condition.
   B. The girls felt bad about the misunderstanding which had arisen
   C. Sitting near the campfire, the old man told John and I about many exciting adventures he had had.
   D. Neither of us is in a position to undertake a task of that magnitude.

   2.____

3. A. The general concluded that one of the three roads would lead to the besieged city.
   B. The children didn't, as a rule, do hardly anything beyond what they were told to do.
   C. The reason the girl gave for her negligence was that she had acted on the spur of the moment.
   D. The daffodils and tulips look beautiful in that blue vase.

   3.____

4. A. If I was ten years older, I should be interested in this work.
   B. Give the prize to whoever has drawn the best picture.
   C. When you have finished reading the book, take it back to the library.
   D. My drawing is as good as or better than yours.

   4.____

5. A. He asked me whether the substance was animal or vegetable.
   B. An apple which is unripe should not be eaten by a child.
   C. That was an insult to me who am your friend.
   D. Some spy must of reported the matter to the enemy.

   5.____

6. A. Limited time makes quoting the entire message impossible.
   B. Who did she say was going?
   C. The girls in your class have dressed more dolls this year than we.
   D. There was such a large amount of books on the floor that I couldn't find a place for my rocking chair.

   6.____

7. A. What with his sleeplessness and his ill health, he was unable to assume any responsibility for the success of the meeting.
   B. If I had been born in February, I should be celebrating my birthday soon.
   C. In order to prevent breakage, she placed a sheet of paper between each of the plates when she packed them.
   D. After the spring shower, the violets smelled very sweet.

   7.____

8. A. He had laid the book down very reluctantly before the end of the lesson. 8.____
   B. The dog, I am sorry to say, had lain on the bed all night.
   C. The cloth was first lain on a flat surface; then it was pressed with a hot iron.
   D. While we were in Florida, we lay in the sun until we were noticeably tanned.

9. A. If John was in New York during the recent holiday season, I have no doubt he spent most of the time with his parents. 9.____
   B. How could he enjoy the television program; the dog was barking and the baby was crying.
   C. When the problem was explained to the class, he must have been asleep.
   D. She wished that her new dress were finished so that she could go to the party.

10. A. The engine not only furnishes power but light and heat as well. 10.____
    B. You're aware that we've forgotten whose guilt was established, aren't you?
    C. Everybody knows that the woman made many sacrifices for her children.
    D. A man with his dog and gun is a familiar sight in this neighborhood.

KEY (CORRECT ANSWERS)

1.	D	6.	D
2.	C	7.	B
3.	B	8.	C
4.	A	9.	B
5.	D	10.	A

TEST 5

DIRECTIONS: Each of Questions 1 through 5 consists of a sentence which may be classified appropriately under one of the following four categories:

A. *Incorrect* because of faulty grammar
B. *Incorrect* because of faulty punctuation
C. *Incorrect* because of faulty spelling
D. *Correct*

Examine each sentence carefully. Then, print in the space at the right the letter preceding the category which is the BEST of the four suggested above

(Note: Each incorrect sentence contains only one type of error. Consider a sentence correct if it contains no errors, although there may be other correct ways of writing the sentence.)

1. Of the two employees, the one in our office is the most efficient. 1.____

2. No one can apply or even understand, the new rules and regulations. 2.____

3. A large amount of supplies were stored in the empty office. 3.____

4. If an employee is occassionally asked to work overtime, he should do so willingly. 4.____

5. It is true that the new procedures are difficult to use but, we are certain that you will learn them quickly. 5.____

6. The office manager said that he did not know who would be given a large allotment under the new plan. 6.____

7. It was at the supervisor's request that the clerk agreed to postpone his vacation. 7.____

8. We do not believe that it is necessary for both he and the clerk to attend the conference. 8.____

9. All employees, who display perseverance, will be given adequate recognition. 9.____

10. He regrets that some of us employees are dissatisfied with our new assignments. 10.____

11. "Do you think that the raise was merited," asked the supervisor? 11.____

12. The new manual of procedure is a valuable supplament to our rules and regulations. 12.____

13. The typist admitted that she had attempted to pursuade the other employees to assist her in her work. 13.____

14. The supervisor asked that all amendments to the regulations be handled by you and I. 14.____

15. The custodian seen the boy who broke the window. 15.____

KEY (CORRECT ANSWERS)

1.	A	6.	D	11.	B
2.	B	7.	D	12.	C
3.	A	8.	A	13.	C
4.	C	9.	B	14.	A
5.	B	10.	D	15.	A

PREPARING WRITTEN MATERIAL

PARAGRAPH REARRANGEMENT COMMENTARY

The sentences that follow are in scrambled order. You are to rearrange them in proper order and indicate the letter choice containing the correct answer at the space at the right.

Each group of sentences in this section is actually a paragraph presented in scrambled order. Each sentence in the group has a place in that paragraph; no sentence is to be left out. You are to read each group of sentences and decide upon the best order in which to put the sentences so as to form a well-organized paragraph.

The questions in this section measure the ability to solve a problem when all the facts relevant to its solution are not given.

More specifically, certain positions of responsibility and authority require the employee to discover connection between events sometimes, apparently, unrelated. In order to do this, the employee will find it necessary to correctly infer that unspecified events have probably occurred or are likely to occur. This ability becomes especially important when action must be taken on incomplete information.

Accordingly, these questions require competitors to choose among several suggested alternatives, each of which presents a different sequential arrangement of the events. Competitors must choose the MOST logical of the suggested sequences.

In order to do so, they may be required to draw on general knowledge to infer missing concepts or events that are essential to sequencing the given events. Competitors should be careful to infer only what is essential to the sequence. The plausibility of the wrong alternatives will always require the inclusion of unlikely events or of additional chains of events which are NOT essential to sequencing the given events.

It's very important to remember that you are looking for the best of the four possible choices, and that the best choice of all may not even be one of the answers you're given to choose from.

There is no one right way to solve these problems. Many people have found it helpful to first write out the order of the sentences, as they would have arranged them, on their scrap paper before looking at the possible answers. If their optimum answer is there, this can save them some time. If it isn't, this method can still give insight into solving the problem. Others find it most helpful to just go through each of the possible choices, contrasting each as they go along. You should use whatever method feels comfortable and works for you.

While most of these types of questions are not that difficult, we've added a higher percentage of the difficult type, just to give you more practice. Usually there are only one or two questions on this section that contain such subtle distinctions that you're unable to answer confidently. And you then may find yourself stuck deciding between two possible choices, neither of which you're sure about.

EXAMINATION SECTION

TEST 1

DIRECTIONS: The following groups of sentences need to be arranged in an order that makes sense. Select the letter preceding the sequence that represents the BEST sentence order. *PRINT THE LETTER OF THE CORRECT ANSWER IN THE SPACE AT THE RIGHT.*

1. I. The keyboard was purposely designed to be a little awkward to slow typists down. 1.____
   II. The arrangement of letters on the keyboard of a typewriter was not designed for the convenience of the typist.
   III. Fortunately, no one is suggesting that a new keyboard be designed right away.
   IV. If one were, we would have to learn to type all over again.
   V. The reason was that the early machines were slower than the typists and would jam easily.

   The CORRECT answer is:
   A. I, III, IV, II, V
   B. II, V, I, IV, III
   C. V, I, II, III, IV
   D. II, I, V, III, IV

2. I. The majority of the new service jobs are part-time or low-paying. 2.____
   II. According to the U.S. Bureau of Labor Statistics, jobs in the service sector constitute 72% of all jobs in this country.
   III. If more and more workers receive less and less money, who will buy the goods and services needed to keep the economy going?
   IV. The service sector is by far the fastest growing part of the United States economy.
   V. Some economists look upon this trend with great concern.

   The CORRECT answer is:
   A. II, IV, I, V, III
   B. II, III, IV, I, V
   C. V, IV, II, III, I
   D. III, I, II, IV, V

3. I. They can also affect one's endurance. 3.____
   II. This can stabilize blood sugar levels, and ensure that the brain is receiving a steady, constant, supply of glucose, so that one is *hitting on all cylinders* while taking the test.
   III. By food, we mean real food, not junk food or unhealthy snacks.
   IV. For this reason, it is important not to skip a meal, and to bring food with you to the exam.
   V. One's blood sugar levels can affect how clearly one is able to think and concentrate during an exam.

   The CORRECT answer is:
   A. V, IV, II, III, I
   B. V, II, I, IV, III
   C. V, I, IV, III, II
   D. V, IV, I, III, II

4. I. Those who are the embodiment of desire are absorbed in material quests, and those who are the embodiment of feeling are warriors who value power more than possession.
   II. These qualities are in everyone, but in different degrees.
   III. But those who value understanding yearn not for goods or victory, but for knowledge.
   IV. According to Plato, human behavior flows from three main sources: desire, emotion, and knowledge.
   V. In the perfect state, the industrial forces would produce but not rule, the military would protect but not rule, and the forces of knowledge, the philosopher kings, would reign.

   The CORRECT answer is:
   A. IV, V, I, II, III
   B. V, I, II, III, IV
   C. IV, III, II, I, V
   D. IV, II, I, III, V

4.____

5. I. Of the more than 26,000 tons of garbage produced daily in New York City, 12,000 tons arrive daily at Fresh Kills.
   II. In a month, enough garbage accumulates there to fill the Empire State Building.
   III. In 1937, the Supreme Court halted the practice of dumping the trash of New York City into the sea.
   IV. Although the garbage is compacted, in a few years the mounds of garbage at Fresh Kills will be the highest points south of Maine's Mount Desert Island on the Eastern Seaboard.
   V. Instead, tugboats now pull barges of much of the trash to Staten Island and the largest landfill in the world, Fresh Kills.

   The CORRECT answer is:
   A. III, V, IV, I, II
   B. III, V, II, IV, I
   C. III, V, I, II, IV
   D. III, II, V, IV, I

5.____

6. I. Communists rank equality very high, but freedom very low.
   II. Unlike communists, conservatives place a high value on freedom and a very low value on equality.
   III. A recent study demonstrated that one way to classify people's political beliefs is to look at the importance placed on two words: freedom and equality.
   IV. Thus, by demonstrating how members of these groups feel about the two words, the study has proved to be useful for political analysts in several European countries.
   V. According to the study, socialists and liberals rank both freedom and equality very high, while fascists rate both very low.

   The CORRECT answer is:
   A. III, V, I, II, IV
   B. V, IV, III, I, II
   C. III, V, IV, II, I
   D. III, I, II, IV, V

6.____

7. I. "Can there be anything more amazing than this?"
   II. If the riddle is successfully answered, his dead brothers will be brought back to life.
   III. "Even though man sees those around him dying every day," says Dharmaraj, "he still believes and acts as if he were immortal."
   IV. "What is the cause of ceaseless wonder?" asks the Lord of the Lake.
   V. In the ancient epic, The Mahabharata, a riddle is asked of one of the Pandava brothers.

   The CORRECT answer is:
   A. V, II, I, IV, III
   B. V, IV, III, I, II
   C. V, II, IV, III, I
   D. V, II, IV, I, III

7.____

8. I. On the contrary, the two main theories—the cooperative (neoclassical) theory and the radical (labor theory)—clearly rest on very different assumptions, which have very different ethical overtones.
   II. The distribution of income is the primary factor in determining the relative levels of material well-being that different groups or individuals attain.
   III. Of all issues in economics, the distribution of income is one of the most controversial.
   IV. The neoclassical theory tends to support the existing income distribution (or minor changes), while the labor theory ends to support substantial changes in the way income is distributed.
   V. The intensity of the controversy reflects the fact that different economic theories are not purely neutral, *detached* theories with no ethical or moral implications.

   The CORRECT answer is:
   A. II, I, V, IV, III
   B. III, II, V, I, IV
   C. III, V, II, I, IV
   D. III, V, IV, I, II

8.____

9. I. The pool acts as a broker and ensures that the cheapest power gets used first.
   II. Every six seconds, the pool's computer monitors all of the generating stations in the state and decides which to ask for more power and which to cut back.
   III. The buying and selling of electrical power is handled by the New York Power Pool in Guilderland, New York.
   IV. This is to the advantage of both the buying and selling utilities.
   V. The pool began operation in 1970, and consists of the state's eight electric utilities.

   The CORRECT answer is:
   A. V, I, II, III, IV
   B. IV, II, I, III, V
   C. III, V, I, IV, II
   D. V, III, IV, II, I

9.____

10. I. Modern English is much simpler grammatically than Old English. 10.____
    II. Finnish grammar is very complicated; there are some fifteen cases, for example.
    III. Chinese, a very old language, may seem to be the exception, but it is the great number of characters/words that must be mastered that makes it so difficult to learn, not its grammar.
    IV. The newest literary language—that is, written as well as spoken—is Finish, whose literary roots go back only to about the middle of the nineteenth century.
    V. Contrary to popular belief, the longer a language is been in use the simpler its grammar—not the reverse.

    The CORRECT answer is:
    A. IV, I, II, III, V
    B. V, I, IV, II, III
    C. I, II, IV, III, V
    D. IV, II, III, I, V

KEY (CORRECT ANSWERS)

1.	D	6.	A
2.	A	7.	C
3.	C	8.	B
4.	D	9.	C
5.	C	10.	B

TEST 2

DIRECTIONS: This type of question tests your ability to recognize accurate paraphrasing, well-constructed paragraphs, and appropriate style and tone. It is important that the answer you select contains only the facts or concepts given in the original sentences. It is also important that you be aware of incomplete sentences, inappropriate transitions, unsupported opinions, incorrect usage, and illogical sentence order. Paragraphs that do not include all the necessary facts and concepts, that distort them, or that add new ones are not considered correct.

The format for this section may vary. Sometimes, long paragraphs are given, and emphasis is placed on style and organization. Our first five questions are of this type. Other times, the paragraphs are shorter, and there is less emphasis on style and more emphasis on accurate representation of information. Our second group of five questions are of this nature.

For each of Questions 1 through 10, select the paragraph that BEST expresses the ideas contained in the sentences above it. *PRINT THE LETTER OF THE CORRECT ANSWER IN THE SPACE AT THE RIGHT.*

1. I. Listening skills are very important for managers. 1.____
   II. Listening skills are not usually emphasized.
   III. Whenever managers are depicted in books, manuals or the media, they are always talking, never listening.
   IV. We'd like you to read the enclosed handout on listening skills and to try to consciously apply them this week.
   V. We guarantee they will improve the quality of your interactions.

   A. Unfortunately, listening skills are not usually emphasized for managers. Managers are always depicted as talking, never listening. We'd like you to read the enclosed handout on listening skills. Please try to apply these principles this week. If you do, we guarantee they will improve the quality of your interactions.
   B. The enclosed handout on listening skills will be important improving the quality of your interactions. We guarantee it. All you have to do is take sometime this week to read and to consciously try to apply the principles. Listening skills are very important for manages, but they are not usually emphasized. Whenever managers are depicted in books, manuals or the media, they are always talking, never listening.
   C. Listening well is one of the most important skills a manager can have, yet it's not usually given much attention. Think about any representation of managers in books, manuals, or in the media that you may have seen. They're always talking, never listening. We'd like you to read the enclosed handout on listening skills and consciously try to apply them the rest of the week. We guarantee you will see a difference in the quality of your interactions.

D. Effective listening, one very important tool in the effective manager's arsenal, is usually not emphasized enough. The usual depiction of managers in books, manuals or the media is one in which they are always talking, never listening. We'd like you to read the enclosed handout and consciously try to apply the information contained therein throughout the rest of the week. We feel sure that you will see a marked difference in the quality of your interactions.

2. I. Chekhov wrote three dramatic masterpieces which share certain themes and formats: Uncle Vanya, The Cherry Orchard, and The Three Sisters. 2.____
II. They are primarily concerned with the passage of time and how this erodes human aspirations.
III. The plays are haunted by the ghosts of the wasted life.
IV. The characters are concerned with life's lesser problems; however, such as the inability to make decisions, loyalty to the wrong cause, and the inability to be clear.
V. This results in sweet, almost aching, type of a sadness referred to as Chekhovian.

A. Chekhov wrote three dramatic masterpieces: Uncle Vanya, The Cherry Orchard, and The Three Sisters. These masterpieces share certain themes and formats: the passage of time, how time erodes human aspirations, and the ghosts of wasted life. Each masterpiece is characterized by a sweet, almost aching, type of sadness that has become known as Chekhovian. The sweetness of this sadness hinges on the fact that it is not the great tragedies of life which are destroying these characters, but their minor flaws: indecisiveness, misplaced loyalty, unclarity.
B. The Cherry Orchard, Uncle Vanya, and The Three Sisters are three dramatic masterpieces written by Chekhov that use similar formats to explore a common theme. Each is primarily concerned with the way that passing time wears down human aspirations, and each is haunted by the ghosts of the wasted life. The characters are shown struggling futilely with the lesser problems of life: indecisiveness, loyalty to the wrong cause, and the inability to be clear. These struggles create a mood of sweet, almost aching, sadness that has become known as Chekhovian.
C. Chekhov's dramatic masterpieces are, along with The Cherry Orchard, Uncle Vanya, and The Three Sisters. These plays share certain thematic and formal similarities. They are concerned most of all with the passage of time and the way in which time erodes human aspirations. Each play is haunted by the specter of the wasted life. Chekhov's characters are caught, however, by life's lesser snares: indecisiveness, loyalty to the wrong cause, and unclarity. The characteristic mood is a sweet, almost aching type of sadness that has come to be known as Chekhovian.
D. A Chekhovian mood is characterized by sweet, almost aching, sadness. The term comes from three dramatic tragedies by Chekhov which revolve around the sadness of a wasted life. The three masterpieces (Uncle Vanya, The Three Sisters, and The Cherry Orchard) share the same

theme and format. The plays are concerned with how the passage of time erodes human aspirations. They are peopled with characters who are struggling with life's lesser problems. These are people who are indecisive, loyal to the wrong causes, or are unable to make themselves clear.

3. I. Movie previews have often helped producers decide which parts of movies they should take out or leave in.
   II. The first 1933 preview of King Kong was very helpful to the producers because many people ran screaming from the theater and would not return when four men first attacked by Kong were eaten by giant spiders.
   III. The 1950 premiere of Sunset Boulevard resulted in the filming of an entirely new beginning, and a delay of six months in the film's release.
   IV. In the original opening scene, William Holden was in a morgue talking with thirty-six other "corpses" about the ways some of them had died.
   V. When he began to tell them of his life with Gloria Swanson, the audience found this hilarious, instead of taking the scene seriously.

3.____

A. Movie previews have often helped producers decide what parts of movies they should leave in or take out. For example, the first preview of King Kong in 1933 was very helpful. In one scene, four men were first attacked by Kong and then eaten by giant spiders. Many members of the audience ran screaming from the theater and would not return. The premiere of the 1950 film Sunset Boulevard was also very helpful. In the original opening scene, William Holden was in a morgue with thirty-six other "corpses," discussing the ways some of them had died. When he began to tell them of his life with Gloria Swanson, the audience found this hilarious. They were supposed to take the scene seriously. The result was a delay of six months in the release of the film while a new beginning was added.

B. Movie previews have often helped producers decide whether they should change various parts of a movie. After the 1933 preview of King Kong, a scene in which four men who had been attacked by Kong were eaten by giant spiders was taken out as many people ran screaming from the theater and would not return. The 1950 premiere of Sunset Boulevard also led to some changes. In the original opening scene, William Holden was in a morgue talking with thirty-six other "corpses" about the ways some of them had died. When he began to tell them of his life with Gloria Swanson, the audience found this hilarious, instead of taking the scene seriously.

C. What do Sunset Boulevard and King Kong have in common? Both show the value of using movie previews to test audience reaction. The first 1933 preview of King Kong showed that a scene showing four men being eaten by giant spiders after having been attacked by Kong was too frightening for many people. They ran screaming from the theater and couldn't be coaxed back. The 1950 premiere of Sunset Boulevard was also a scream, but not the kind the producers intended. The movie opens with William Holden lying in a morgue discussing the ways they had died with thirty-six other "corpses." When he began to tell them of his life with Gloria Swanson, the audience couldn't take him seriously. Their laughter caused a six-month delay while the beginning was rewritten.

D. Producers very often use movie previews to decide if changes are needed. The premiere of Sunset Boulevard in 1950 led to a new beginning and a six-month delay in film release. At the beginning, William Holden and thirty-six other "corpses" discuss the ways some of them died. Rather than taking this seriously, the audience thought it was hilarious when he began to tell them of his life with Gloria Swanson. The first 1933 preview of King Kong was very helpful for its producers because one scene so terrified the audience that many of them ran screaming from the theater and would not return. In this particular scene, four men who had first been attacked by Kong were eaten by giant spiders.

4. I. It is common for supervisors to view employees as "things" to be manipulated. 4.____

II. This approach does not motivate employees, nor does the carrot-and-stick approach because employees often recognize these behaviors and resent them.

III. Supervisors can change these behaviors by using self-inquiry and persistence.

IV. The best managers genuinely respect those they work with, are supportive and helpful, and are interested in working as a team with those they supervise.

V. They disagree with the Golden Rule that says "he or she who has the gold makes the rules."

A. Some managers act as if they think the Golden Rule means "he or she who has the gold makes the rules." They show disrespect to employees by seeing them as "things" to be manipulated. Obviously, this approach does not motivate employees any more than the carrot-and-stick approach motivates them. The employees are smart enough to spot these behaviors and resent them. On the other hand, the managers genuinely respect those they work with, are supportive and helpful, and are interested in working as a team. Self-inquiry and persistence can change even the former type of supervisor into the latter.

B. Many supervisors all into the trap of viewing employees as "things" to be manipulated, or try to motivate them by using a carrot-and-stick approach. These methods do not motivate employees, who often recognize the behaviors and resent them. Supervisors can change these behaviors, however, by using self-inquiry and persistence. The best managers are supportive and helpful, and have genuine respect for those with whom they work. They are interested in working as a team with those they supervise. To them, the Golden Rule is not "he or she who has the gold makes the rules."

C. Some supervisors see employees as "things" to be used or manipulated using a carrot-and-stick technique. These methods don't work. Employees often see through them and resent them. A supervisor who wants to change may do so. The techniques of self-inquiry and persistence can be used to turn him or her into the type of supervisor who doesn't think the Golden Rule is "he or she who has the gold makes the rules." They may become like the best managers who treat those with whom they work with respect and give them help and support. These are the manager who know how to build a team.

D. Unfortunately, many supervisors act as if their employees are objects whose movements they can position at will. This mistaken belief has the same result as another popular motivational technique—the carrot-and-stick approach. Both attitudes can lead to the same result—resentment from those employees who recognize the behaviors for what they are. Supervisors who recognize these behaviors can change through the use of persistence and the use of self-inquiry. It's important to remember that the best managers respect their employees. They readily give necessary help and support and are interested in working as a team with those they supervise. To these managers, the Golden Rule is not "he or she who has the gold makes the rules."

5. I. The first half of the nineteenth century produced a group of pessimistic poets—Byron, De Musset, Heine, Pushkin, and Leopardi. 5.____

II. It also produced a group of pessimistic composers—Schubert, Chopin, Schumann, and even the later Beethoven.

III. Above all, in philosophy, there was the profoundly pessimistic philosopher, Schopenhauer.

IV. The Revolution was dead, the Bourbons were restored, the feudal barons were reclaiming their land, and progress everywhere was being suppressed, as the great age was over.

V. "I thank God," said Goethe, "that I am not young in so thoroughly finished a world."

A. "I thank God," said Goethe, "that I am not young in so thoroughly finished a world." The Revolution was dead, the Bourbons were restored, the feudal barons were reclaiming their land, and progress everywhere was being suppressed. The first half of the nineteenth century produced a group of pessimistic poets: Byron, De Musset, Heine, Pushkin, and Leopardi. It also produced pessimistic composers: Schubert, Chopin, Schumann. Although Beethoven came later, he fits into this group, too. Finally and above all, it also produced a profoundly pessimistic philosopher, Schopenhauer. The great age was over.

B. The first half of the nineteenth century produced a group of pessimistic poets: Byron, De Musset, Heine, Pushkin, and Leopardi. It produced a group of pessimistic composers: Schubert, Chopin, Schumann, and even the later Beethoven. Above all, it produced a profoundly pessimistic philosopher, Schopenhauer. For each of these men, the great age was over. The Revolution was dead, and the Bourbons were restored. The feudal barons were reclaiming their land, and progress everywhere was being suppressed.

C. The great age was over. The Revolution was dead—the Bourbons were restored, and the feudal barons were reclaiming their land. Progress everywhere was being suppressed. Out of this climate came a profound pessimism. Poets, like Byron, De Musset, Heine, Pushkin, and Leopardi; composers, like Schubert, Chopin, Schumann, and even the later Beethoven; and above all, a profoundly pessimistic philosopher, Schopenauer. This pessimism which arose in the first half of the nineteenth century is illustrated by these words of Goethe, "I thank God that I am not young in so thoroughly finished a world."

D. The first half of the nineteenth century produced a group of pessimistic poets, Byron, De Musset, Heine, Pushkin, and Leopardi—and a group of pessimistic composers, Schubert, Chopin, Schumann, and the later Beethoven. Above it all, it produced a profoundly pessimistic philosopher, Schopenhauer. The great age was over. The Revolution was dead, the Bourbons were restored, the feudal barons were reclaiming their land, and progress everywhere was being suppressed. "I thank God," said Goethe, "that I am not young in so thoroughly finished a world."

6. I. A new manager sometimes may feel insecure about his or her competence in the new position. 6.____

II. The new manager may then exhibit defensive or arrogant behavior towards those one supervises, or the new manager may direct overly flattering behavior toward one's new supervisor.

A. Sometimes, a new manager may feel insecure about his or her ability to perform well in this new position. The insecurity may lead him or her to treat others differently. He or she may display arrogant or defensive behavior towards those he or she supervises, or be overly flattering to his or her new supervisor.

B. A new manager may sometimes feel insecure about his or her ability to perform well in the new position. He or she may then become arrogant, defensive, or overly flattering towards those he or she works with.

C. There are times when a new manager may be insecure about how well he or she can perform in the new job. The new manager may also behave defensive or act in an arrogant way towards those he or she supervises, or overly flatter his or her boss.

D. Sometimes a new manager may feel insecure about his or her ability to perform well in the new position. He or she may then display arrogant or defensive behavior towards those they supervise, or become overly flattering towards their supervisors.

7. I. It is possible to eliminate unwanted behavior by bringing it under stimulus control—tying the behavior to a cue, and then never, or rarely, giving the cue. 7.____

II. One trainer successfully used this method to keep an energetic young porpoise from coming out of her tank whenever she felt like it, which was potentially dangerous.

III. Her trainer taught her to do it for a reward, in response to a hand signal, and then rarely gave the signal.

A. Unwanted behavior can be eliminated by tying the behavior to a cue, and then never, or rarely, giving the cue. This is called stimulus control. One trainer was able to use this method to keep an energetic young porpoise from coming out of her tank by teaching her to come out for a reward in response to a hand signal, and then rarely giving the signal.
B. Stimulus control can be used to eliminate unwanted behavior. In this method, behavior is tied to a cue, and then the cue is rarely, if ever, given. One trainer was able to successfully use stimulus control to keep an energetic young porpoise from coming out of her tank whenever she felt like it—a potentially dangerous practice. She taught the porpoise to come out for a reward when she gave a hand signal, and then rarely gave the signal.
C. It is possible to eliminate behavior that is undesirable by bringing it under stimulus control by tying behavior to a signal, and then rarely giving the signal. One trainer successfully used this method to keep an energetic porpoise from coming out of her tank, a potentially dangerous situation. Her trainer taught the porpoise to do it for a reward, in response to a hand signal, and then would rarely give the signal.
D. By using stimulus control, it is possible to eliminate unwanted behavior by tying the behavior to a cue, and then rarely or never give the cue. One trainer was able to use this method to successfully stop a young porpoise from coming out of her tank whenever she felt like it. To curb this potentially dangerous practice, the porpoise was taught by the trainer to come out of the tank for a reward, in response to a hand signal, and then rarely given the signal.

8. I. There is a great deal of concern over the safety of commercial trucks, caused by their greatly increased role in serious accidents since federal deregulation in 1981. 8.____
II. Recently, 60 percent of trucks in New York and Connecticut and 70 percent of trucks in Maryland randomly stopped by state troopers failed safety inspections.
III. Sixteen states in the United States require no training at all for truck drivers.

A. Since federal deregulation in 1981, there has been a great deal of concern over the safety of commercial trucks, and their greatly increased role in serious accidents. Recently, 60 percent of trucks in New York and Connecticut, and 70 percent of trucks in Maryland failed safety inspections. Sixteen states in the United States require no training at all for truck drivers.
B. There is a great deal of concern over the safety of commercial trucks since federal deregulation in 1981. Their role in serious accidents has greatly increased. Recently, 60 percent of trucks randomly stopped in Connecticut and New York and 70 percent in Maryland failed safety inspections conducted by state troopers. Sixteen states in the United States provide no training at all for truck drivers.
C. Commercial trucks have a greatly increased role in serious accidents since federal deregulation in 1981. This has led to a great deal of concern.

Recently, 70 percent of trucks in Maryland and 60 percent of trucks in New York and Connecticut failed inspection of those that were randomly stopped by state troopers. Sixteen states in the United States require no training for all truck drivers.

D. Since federal deregulation in 1981, the role that commercial trucks have played in serious accidents has greatly increased, and this has led to a great deal of concern. Recently, 60 percent of trucks in New York and Connecticut, and 70 percent of trucks in Maryland randomly stopped by state troopers failed safety inspections. Sixteen states in the U.S. don't require any training for truck drivers.

9. I. No matter how much some people have, they still feel unsatisfied and want more, or want to keep what they have forever. 9.____

II. One recent television documentary showed several people flying from New York to Paris for a one-day shopping spree to buy platinum earrings, because they were bored.

III. In Brazil, some people were ordering coffins that cost a minimum of $45,000 and are equipping them with deluxe stereos, televisions, and other graveyard necessities.

A. Some people, despite having a great deal, still feel unsatisfied and want more, or think they can keep what they have forever. One recent documentary on television showed several people enroute from Paris to New York for a one day shopping spree to buy platinum earrings, because they were bored. Some people in Brazil are even ordering coffins equipped with such graveyard necessities as deluxe stereos and televisions. The price of the coffins start at $45,000.

B. No matter how much some people have, they may feel unsatisfied. This leads them to want more, or to want to keep what they have forever. Recently, a television documentary depicting several people flying from New York to Paris for a one day shopping spree to buy platinum earrings. They were bored. Some people in Brazil are ordering coffins that cost at least $45,000 and come equipped with deluxe televisions, stereos and other necessary graveyard items.

C. Some people will be dissatisfied no matter how much they have. They may want more, or they may want to keep what they have forever. One recent television documentary showed several people, motivated by boredom, jetting from New York to Paris for a one-day shopping spree to buy platinum earrings. In Brazil, some people are ordering coffins equipped with deluxe stereos, televisions and other graveyard necessities. The minimum price for these coffins—$45,000.

D. Some people are never satisfied. No matter how much they have they still want more, or think they can keep what they have forever. One television documentary recently showed several people flying from New York to Paris for the day to buy platinum earrings because they were bored. In Brazil, some people are ordering coffins that cost $45,000 and are equipped with deluxe stereos, televisions and other graveyard necessities.

10. I. A television signal or video signal has three parts. 10.____
    II. Its parts are the black-and-white portion, the color portion, and the synchronizing (sync) pulses, which keep the picture stable.
    III. Each video source, whether it's a camera or a video-cassette recorder contains its own generator of these synchronizing pulses to accompany the picture that it's sending in order to keep it steady and straight.
    IV. In order to produce a clean recording, a video-cassette recorder must "lock-up" to the sync pulses that are part of the video it is trying to record, and this effort may be very noticeable if the device does not have gunlock.

    A. There are three parts to a television or video signal: the black-and-white part, the color part, and the synchronizing (sync) pulses, which keep the picture stable. Whether it's a video-cassette recorder or a camera, each video source contains its own pulse that synchronizes and generates the picture it's sending in order to keep it straight and steady. A video-cassette recorder must "lock up" to the sync pulses that are part of the video it's trying to record. If the device doesn't have gunlock, this effort must be very noticeable.
    B. A video signal or television is comprised of three parts: the black-and-white portion, the color portion, and the sync (synchronizing) pulses, which keep the picture stable. Whether it's a camera or a video-cassette recorder, each video source contains its own generator of these synchronizing pulses. These accompany the picture that it's sending in order to keep it straight and steady. A video-cassette recorder must "lock up" to the sync pulses that are part of the video it is trying to record in order to produce a clean recording. This effort may be very noticeable if the device does not have gunlock.
    C. There are three parts to a television or video signal: the color portion, the black-and-white portion, and the sync (synchronizing pulses). These keep the picture stable. Each video source, whether it's a video-cassette recorder or a camera, generates these synchronizing pulses accompanying the picture it's sending in order to keep it straight and steady. If a clean recording is to be produced, a video-cassette recorder must store the sync pulses that are part of the video it is trying to record. This effort may not be noticeable if the device does not have gunlock.
    D. A television signal or video signal has three parts: the black-and-white portion, the color portion, and the synchronizing (sync) pulses. It's the sync pulses which keep the picture stable, which accompany it and keep it steady and straight. Whether it's a camera or a video-cassette recorder, each video source contains its own generator of these synchronizing pulses. To produce a clean recording, a video-cassette recorder must "lock up" to the sync pulses that are part of the video it is trying to record. If the device does not have gunlock, this effort may be very noticeable.

KEY (CORRECT ANSWERS)

1.	C	6.	A
2.	B	7.	B
3.	A	8.	D
4.	B	9.	C
5.	D	10.	D

EXAMINATION SECTION

TEST 1

DIRECTIONS: Each question or incomplete statement is followed by several suggested answers or completions. Select the one that BEST answers the question or completes the statement. *PRINT THE LETTER OF THE CORRECT ANSWER IN THE SPACE AT THE RIGHT.*

1. Which one of the following generalizations is MOST likely to be INACCURATE and lead to judgmental errors in communication? 1.____
   A. A supervisor must be able to read with understanding.
   B. Misunderstanding may lead to dislike.
   C. Anyone can listen to another person and understand what he means.
   D. It is usually desirable to let a speaker talk until he is finished.

2. Assume that, as a supervisor, you have been directed to inform your subordinates about the implementation of a new procedure which will affect their work. 2.____
   While communicating this information, you should do all of the following EXCEPT
   A. obtain the approval of your subordinates regarding the new procedure
   B. explain the reason for implementing the new procedure
   C. hold a staff meeting at a time convenient to most of your subordinates
   D. encourage a productive discussion of the new procedure

3. Assume that you are in charge of a section that handles requests for information on matters received from the public. One day, you observe that a clerk under your supervision is using a method to log-in requests for information that is different from the one specified by you in the past. Upon questioning the clerk, you discover that instructions changing the old procedure were delivered orally by your supervisor on a day on which you were absent from the office. 3.____
   Of the following, the MOST appropriate action for you to take is to
   A. tell the clerk to revert to the old procedure at once
   B. ask your supervisor for information about the change
   C. call your staff together and tell them that no existing procedure is to be changed unless you direct that it be done
   D. write a memo to your supervisor suggesting that all future changes in procedure are to be in writing and that they be directed to you

4. At the first meeting with your staff after appointment as a supervisor, you find considerable indifference and some hostility among the participants. 4.____
   Of the following, the MOST appropriate way to handle this situation is to
   A. disregard the attitudes displayed and continue to make your presentation until you have completed it
   B. discontinue your presentation but continue the meeting and attempt to find out the reasons for their attitudes

C. warm up your audience with some good-natured statements and anecdotes and then proceed with your presentation
D. discontinue the meeting and set up personal interviews with the staff members to try to find out the reason for their attitude

5. In order to start the training of a new employee, it has been a standard practice to have him read a manual of instructions or procedures.
This method is currently being replaced by the ______ method.
A. audio-visual
B. conference
C. lecture
D. programmed instruction

5.____

6. Of the following subjects, the one that can usually be successfully taught by a first-line supervisor who is training his subordinates is:
A. theory and philosophy of management
B. human relations
C. responsibilities of a supervisor
D. job skills

6.____

7. Assume that as supervisor you are training a clerk who is experiencing difficulty learning a new task.
Which of the following would be the LEAST effective approach to take when trying to solve this problem? To
A. ask questions which will reveal the clerk's understanding of the task
B. take a different approach in explaining the task
C. give the clerk an opportunity to ask questions about the task
D. make sure the clerk knows you are watching his work closely

7.____

8. One school of management and supervision involves participation by employees in the setting of group goals and in the sharing of responsibility for the operation of the unit.
If this philosophy were applied to a unit consisting of professional and clerical personnel, one should expect
A. the professional and clerical personnel to participate with equal effectiveness in operating areas and policy areas
B. the professional personnel to participate with greater effectiveness than the clerical personnel in policy areas
C. the clerical personnel to participate with greater effectiveness than the professional personnel in operating areas
D. greater participation by clerical personnel but with less responsibility for their actions

8.____

9. With regard to productivity, high morale among employees generally indicates a
A. history of high productivity
B. nearly absolute positive correlation with high productivity
C. predisposition to be productive under facilitating leadership and circumstances
D. complacency which has little effect on productivity

9.____

10. Assume that you are going to organize the professionals and clerks under your supervision into work groups or team of two or three employees. 10.____
Of the following, the step which is LEAST likely to foster the successful development of each group is to
    A. allow friends to work together in the group
    B. provide special help and attention to employees with no friends in their group
    C. frequently switch employees from group to group
    D. rotate jobs within the group in order to strengthen group identification

11. Following are four statements which might be made by an employee to his supervisor during a performance evaluation interview. 11.____
Which of the statements BEST provides a basis for developing a plan to improve the employee's performance?
    A. *I understand that you are dissatisfied with my work and I will try harder in the future.*
    B. *I feel that I've been making too many careless clerical errors recently.*
    C. *I am aware that I will be subject to disciplinary action if my work does not improve within one month.*
    D. *I understand that this interview is simply a requirement of your job and not a personal attack on me.*

12. Three months ago, Mr. Smith and his supervisor, Mrs. Jones, developed a plan which was intended to correct Mr. Smith's inadequate job performance. Now, during a follow-up interview, Mr. Smith, who thought his performance had satisfactorily improved, has been informed that Mrs. Jones is still dissatisfied with his work. 12.____
Of the following, it is MOST likely that the disagreement occurred because, when formulating the plan, they did NOT
    A. set realistic goals for Mr. Smith's performance
    B. set a reasonable time limit for Mr. Smith to effect his improvement in performance
    C. provide for adequate training to improve Mr. Smith's skills
    D. establish performance standards for measuring Mr. Smith's progress

13. When a supervisor delegates authority to subordinates, there are usually many problems to overcome, such as inadequately trained subordinates and poor planning. 13.____
All of the following are means of increasing the effectiveness of delegation EXCEPT:
    A. Defining assignments in the light of results expected
    B. Maintaining open lines of communication
    C. Establishing tight controls so that subordinates will stay within the bounds of the area of delegation
    D. Providing rewards for successful assumption of authority by a subordinate

14. Assume that one of your subordinates has arrived late for work several times during the current month. The last time he was late you had warned him that another unexcused lateness would result informal disciplinary action.
If the employee arrives late for work again during this month, the FIRST action you should take is to
   A. give the employee a chance to explain this lateness
   B. give the employee a written copy of your warning
   C. tell the employee that you are recommending formal disciplinary action
   D. tell the employee that you will give him only one more chance before recommending formal disciplinary action

14.____

15. In trying to decide how many subordinates a manager can control directly, one of the determinants is how much the manager can reduce the frequency and time consumed in contacts with his subordinates.
Of the following, the factor which LEAST influences the number and direction of these contacts is:
   A. How well the manager delegates authority
   B. The rate at which the organization is changing
   C. The control techniques used by the manager
   D. Whether the activity is line or staff

15.____

16. Systematic rotation of employees through lateral transfer within a government organization to provide for managerial development is
   A. *good*, because systematic rotation develops specialists who learn to do many jobs well
   B. *bad*, because the outsider upsets the status quo of the existing organization
   C. *good*, because rotation provides challenge and organizational flexibility
   D. *bad*, because it is upsetting to employees to be transferred within a service

16.____

17. Assume that you are required to provide an evaluation of the performance of your subordinates.
Of the following factors, it is MOST important that the performance evaluation include a rating of each employee's
   A. initiative B. productivity C. intelligence D. personality

17.____

18. When preparing performance evaluations of your subordinates, one way to help assure that you are rating each employee fairly is to
   A. prepare a list of all employees and all the rating factors and rate all employees on one rating factor before going on to the next factor
   B. prepare a list of all your employees and all the rating factors and rate each employee on all factors before going on to the next employee
   C. discuss all the ratings you anticipate giving with another supervisor in order to obtain an unbiased opinion
   D. discuss each employee with his co-workers in order to obtain peer judgment of worth before doing any rating

18.____

19. A managerial plan which would include the GREATEST control is a plan which is 19.____
    A. spontaneous and geared to each new job that is received
    B. detailed and covering an extended time period
    C. long-range and generalized, allowing for various interpretations
    D. specific and prepared daily

20. Assume that you are preparing a report which includes statistical data covering increases in budget allocations of four agencies for the past ten years. 20.____
    For you to represent the statistical data pictorially or graphically within the report is a
    A. *poor* idea, because you should be able to make statistical data understandable through the use of words
    B. *good* idea, because it is easier for the reader to understand pictorial representation rather than quantities of words conveying statistical data
    C. *poor* idea, because using pictorial representation in a report may make the report too expensive to print
    D. *good* idea, because a pictorial representation makes the report appear more attractive than the use of many words to convey the statistical data

---

KEY (CORRECT ANSWERS)

1.	C	11.	A
2.	A	12.	B
3.	B	13.	C
4.	D	14.	A
5.	D	15.	D
6.	D	16.	C
7.	D	17.	B
8.	B	18.	A
9.	C	19.	B
10.	C	20.	B

TEST 2

DIRECTIONS: Each question or incomplete statement is followed by several suggested answers or completions. Select the one that BEST answers the question or completes the statement. *PRINT THE LETTER OF THE CORRECT ANSWER IN THE SPACE AT THE RIGHT.*

1. Research studies have shown that supervisors of groups with high production records USUALLY 1.____
   A. give detailed instructions, constantly check on progress, and insist on approval of all decisions before implementation
   B. do considerable paperwork and other work similar to that performed by subordinates
   C. think of themselves as team members on the same level as others in the work group
   D. perform tasks traditionally associated with managerial functions

2. Mr. Smith, a bureau chief, is summoned by his agency's head in a conference to discuss Mr. Jones, an accountant who works in one of the divisions of his bureau. Mr. Jones has committed an error of such magnitude as to arouse the agency head's concern. 2.____
   After agreeing with the other conferees that a severe reprimand would be the appropriate punishment, Mr. Smith SHOULD
   A. arrange for Mr. Jones to explain the reasons for his error to the agency head
   B. send a memorandum to Mr. Jones, being careful that the language emphasizes the nature of the error rather than Mr. Jones' personal faults
   C. inform Mr. Jones' immediate supervisor of the conclusion reached at the conference, and let the supervisor take the necessary action
   D. suggest to the agency head that no additional action be taken against Mr. Jones because no further damage will be caused by the error

3. Assume that Ms. Thomson, a unit chief, has determined that the findings of an internal audit have been seriously distorted as a result of careless errors. The audit had been performed by a group of auditors in her unit and the errors were overlooked by the associate accountant in charge of the audit. Ms. Thomson has decided to delay discussing the matter with the associate accountant and the staff who performed the audit until she verifies certain details, which may require prolonged investigation. 3.____
   Mrs. Thomson's method of handling this situation is
   A. *appropriate*; employees should not be accused of wrongdoing until all the facts have been determined
   B. *inappropriate*; the employees involved may assume that the errors were considered unimportant
   C. *appropriate*; employees are more likely to change their behavior as a result of disciplinary action taken after a *cooling off* period
   D. *inappropriate*; the employees involved may have forgotten the details and become emotionally upset when confronted with the facts

4. After studying the financial situation in his agency, an administrative accountant decides to recommend centralization of certain accounting functions which are being performed in three different bureaus of the organization
The one of the following which is MOST likely to be a DISADVANTAE if this recommendation is implemented is that
   A. there may be less coordination of the accounting procedure because central direction is not so close to the day-to-day problems as the personnel handling them in each specialized accounting unit
   B. the higher management levels would not be able to make emergency decisions in as timely a manner as the more involved, lower-level administrators who are closer to the problem
   C. it is more difficult to focus the attention of the top management in order to resolve accounting problems because of the many other activities top management is involved in at the same time
   D. the accuracy of upward and inter-unit communication may be reduced because centralization may require insertion of more levels of administration in the chain of command

4.____

5. Of the following assumptions about the role of conflict in an organization, the one which is the MOST accurate statement of the approach of modern management theorists is that conflict
   A. can usually be avoided or controlled
   B. serves as a vital element in organizational change
   C. works against attainment of organizational goals
   D. provides a constructive outlet for problem employees

5.____

6. Which of the following is generally regarded as the BEST approach for a supervisor to follow in handling grievances brought by subordinates?
   A. Avoid becoming involved personally
   B. Involve the union representative in the first stage of discussion
   C. Settle the grievance as soon as possible
   D. Arrange for arbitration by a third party

6.____

7. Assume that supervisors of similar-sized accounting units in city, state, and federal offices were interviewed and observed at their work. It was found that the ways they acted in and viewed their roles tended to be very similar, regardless of who employed them.
Which of the following is the BEST explanation of this similarity
   A. A supervisor will ordinarily behave in conformance to his own self-image.
   B. Each role in an organization, including the supervisory role, calls for a distinct type of personality.
   C. The supervisor role reflects an exceptionally complex pattern of human response.
   D. The general nature of the duties and responsibilities of the supervisory position determines the role.

7.____

8. Which of the following is NOT consistent with the findings of recent research about the characteristics of successful top managers? 8.____
   A. They are *inner-directed* and not overly concerned with pleasing others.
   B. They are challenged by situations filled with high risk and ambiguity.
   C. They tend to stay on the same job for long periods of time.
   D. They consider it more important to handle critical assignments successfully than to do routine work well.

9. As a supervisor, you have to give subordinates operational guidelines. 9.____
   Of the following, the BEST reason for providing them with information about the overall objectives within which their operations fit is that the subordinates will
   A. be more likely to carry out the operation according to your expectations
   B. know that there is a legitimate reason for carrying out the operation in the way you have prescribed
   C. be more likely to handle unanticipated problems that may arise without having to take up your time
   D. more likely to transmit the operating instructions correctly to their subordinates

10. A supervisor holds frequent meetings with his staff. 10.____
    Of the following, the BEST approach he can take in order to elicit productive discussions at these meetings is for him to
    A. ask questions of those who attend
    B. include several levels of supervisors at the meetings
    C. hold the meetings at a specified time each week
    D. begin each meeting with a statement that discussion is welcomed

11. Of the following, the MOST important action that a supervisor can take to increase the productivity of a subordinate is to 11.____
    A. increase his uninterrupted work time
    B. increase the number of reproducing machines available in the office
    C. provide clerical assistance whenever he requests it
    D. reduce the number of his assigned tasks

12. Assume that, as a supervisor, you find out that you often must countermand or modify your original staff memos. 12.____
    If this practice continues, which one of the following situations is MOST likely to occur? The
    A. staff will not bother to read your memos
    B. office files will become cluttered
    C. staff will delay acting on your memos
    D. memos will be treated routinely

13. In making management decisions, the committee approach is often used by managers. 13.____
    Of the following, the BEST reason for using this approach is to
    A. prevent any one individual from assuming too much authority
    B. allow the manager to bring a wider range of experience and judgment to bear on the problem

C. allow the participation of all staff members, which will make them feel more committed to the decisions reached
D. permit the rapid transmission of information about decisions reached to the staff members concerned

14. In establishing standards for the measurement of the performance of a management project team, it is MOST important for the project manager to 14.____
A. identify and define the objectives of the project
B. determine the number of people who will be assigned to the project team
C. evaluate the skills of the staff who will be assigned to the project team
D. estimate fairly accurately the length of time required to complete each phase of the project

15. It is virtually impossible to tell an employee either that he is not good as another employee or that he does not measure up to a desirable level of performance, without having him feel threatened, rejected, and discouraged. 15.____
In accordance with the foregoing observation, a supervisor who is concerned about the performance of the less efficient members of his staff should realize that
A. he might obtain better results by not discussing the quality and quantity of their work with them, but by relying instead on the written evaluation of their performance to motivate their improvement
B. since he is required to discuss their performance with them, he should do so in words of encouragement and in so friendly a manner as to not destroy their morale
C. he might discuss their work in a general way, without mentioning any of the specifics about the quality of their performance, with the expectation that they would understand the full implications of his talk
D. he should make it a point, while telling them of their poor performance, to mention that their work is as good as that of some of the other employees in the unit

16. Some advocates of management-by-objectives procedures in public agencies have been urging that this method of operations be expanded to encompass all agencies of the government, for one or more of the following reasons, not all of which may be correct: 16.____
I. The MBO method is likely to succeed because it embraces the practice of setting near-term goals for the subordinate manager, reviewing accomplishments at an appropriate time, and repeating this process indefinitely
II. Provision for authority to perform the tasks assigned as goals in the MBO method is normally not needed because targets are set in quantitative or qualitative terms and specific times for accomplishment are arranged in short-term, repetitive intervals
III. Many other appraisal-of-performance programs failed because both supervisors and subordinates resisted them, while the MBO approach is not instituted until there is an organizational commitment to it
IV. Personal accountability is clearly established through the MBO approach because verifiable results are set up in the process of formulating the targets

Which of the choices below includes ALL of the foregoing statements that are CORRECT?

A. I, III B. II, IV C. I, II, III, IV D. I, III, IV

17. In preparing an organizational structure, the PRINCIPAL guideline for locating staff units is to place them 17.____
    A. all under a common supervisor
    B. as close as possible to the activities they serve
    C. as close to the chief executive as possible without over-extending his span of control
    D. at the lowest operational level

18. The relative importance of any unit in a department can be LEAST reliably judged by the 18.____
    A. amount of office space allocated to the unit
    B. number of employees in the unit
    C. rank of the individual who heads the unit
    D. rank of the individual to whom the unit head reports directly

19. Those who favor Planning-Programming-Budgeting Systems (PPBS) as a new method of governmental financial administration emphasize that PPBS 19.____
    A. applies statistical measurements which correlate highly with criteria
    B. makes possible economic systems analysis, including an explicit examination of alternatives
    C. makes available scarce government resources which can be coordinated on a government-wide basis and shared between local units of government
    D. shifts the emphasis in budgeting methods to an automated system of data processing

20. The term applied to computer processing which processes data concurrently with a given activity and provides results soon enough to influence the selection of a course of action is _____ processing. 20.____
    A. realtime B. batch
    C. random access D. integrated data

KEY (CORRECT ANSWERS)

1.	D	11.	A
2.	C	12.	C
3.	B	13.	B
4.	D	14.	A
5.	B	15.	B
6.	C	16.	D
7.	D	17.	B
8.	C	18.	B
9.	C	19.	B
10.	A	20.	A

PHILOSOPHY, PRINCIPLES, PRACTICES AND TECHNICS OF SUPERVISION, ADMINISTRATION, MANAGEMENT AND ORGANIZATION

TABLE OF CONTENTS

TABLE OF CONTENTS (CONTINUED)

PHILOSOPHY, PRINCIPLES, PRACTICES, AND TECHNICS
OF
SUPERVISION, ADMINISTRATION, MANAGEMENT AND ORGANIZATION

I. MEANING OF SUPERVISION

The extension of the democratic philosophy has been accompanied by an extension in the scope of supervision. Modern leaders and supervisors no longer think of supervision in the narrow sense of being confined chiefly to visiting employees, supplying materials, or rating the staff. They regard supervision as being intimately related to all the concerned agencies of society, they speak of the supervisor's function in terms of "growth", rather than the "improvement," of employees.

This modern concept of supervision may be defined as follows:

Supervision is leadership and the development of leadership within groups which are cooperatively engaged in inspection, research, training, guidance and evaluation.

II. THE OLD AND THE NEW SUPERVISION

TRADITIONAL

1. Inspection
2. Focused on the employee
3. Visitation
4. Random and haphazard
5. Imposed and authoritarian
6. One person usually

MODERN

1. Study and analysis
2. Focused on aims, materials, methods, supervisors, employees, environment
3. Demonstrations, intervisitation, workshops, directed reading, bulletins, etc.
4. Definitely organized and planned (scientific)
5. Cooperative and democratic
6. Many persons involved (creative)

III THE EIGHT (8) BASIC PRINCIPLES OF THE NEW SUPERVISION

1. *PRINCIPLE OF RESPONSIBILITY*

   Authority to act and responsibility for acting must be joined.

   a. If you give responsibility, give authority.
   b. Define employee duties clearly.
   c. Protect employees from criticism by others.
   d. Recognize the rights as well as obligations of employees.
   e. Achieve the aims of a democratic society insofar as it is possible within the area of your work.
   f. Establish a situation favorable to training and learning.
   g. Accept ultimate responsibility for everything done in your section, unit, office, division, department.
   h. Good administration and good supervision are inseparable.

2. *PRINCIPLE OF AUTHORITY*

The success of the supervisor is measured by the extent to which the power of authority is not used.

a. Exercise simplicity and informality in supervision.
b. Use the simplest machinery of supervision.
c. If it is good for the organization as a whole, it is probably justified.
d. Seldom be arbitrary or authoritative.
e. Do not base your work on the power of position or of personality.
f. Permit and encourage the free expression of opinions.

3. *PRINCIPLE OF SELF-GROWTH*

The success of the supervisor is measured by the extent to which, and the speed with which, he is no longer needed.

a. Base criticism on principles, not on specifics.
b. Point out higher activities to employees.
c. Train for self-thinking by employees, to meet new situations.
d. Stimulate initiative, self-reliance and individual responsibility.
e. Concentrate on stimulating the growth of employees rather than on removing defects.

4. *PRINCIPLE OF INDIVIDUAL WORTH*

Respect for the individual is a paramount consideration in supervision.

a. Be human and sympathetic in dealing with employees.
b. Don't nag about things to be done.
c. Recognize the individual differences among employees and seek opportunities to permit best expression of each personality.

5. *PRINCIPLE OF CREATIVE LEADERSHIP*

The best supervision is that which is not apparent to the employee.

a. Stimulate, don't drive employees to creative action.
b. Emphasize doing good things.
c. Encourage employees to do what they do best.
d. Do not be too greatly concerned with details of subject or method.
e. Do not be concerned exclusively with immediate problems and activities.
f. Reveal higher activities and make them both desired and maximally possible.
g. Determine procedures in the light of each situation but see that these are derived from a sound basic philosophy.
h. Aid, inspire and lead so as to liberate the creative spirit latent in all good employees.

6. *PRINCIPLE OF SUCCESS AND FAILURE*

There are no unsuccessful employees, only unsuccessful supervisors who have failed to give proper leadership.

a. Adapt suggestions to the capacities, attitudes, and prejudices of employees.
b. Be gradual, be progressive, be persistent.
c. Help the employee find the general principle; have the employee apply his own problem to the general principle.
d. Give adequate appreciation for good work and honest effort.
e. Anticipate employee difficulties and help to prevent them.
f. Encourage employees to do the desirable things they will do anyway.
g. Judge your supervision by the results it secures.

7. *PRINCIPLE OF SCIENCE*

Successful supervision is scientific, objective, and experimental. It is based on facts, not on prejudices.

a. Be cumulative in results.
b. Never divorce your suggestions from the goals of training.
c. Don't be impatient of results.
d. Keep all matters on a professional, not a personal level.
e. Do not be concerned exclusively with immediate problems and activities.
f. Use objective means of determining achievement and rating where possible.

8. *PRINCIPLE OF COOPERATION*

Supervision is a cooperative enterprise between supervisor and employee.

a. Begin with conditions as they are.
b. Ask opinions of all involved when formulating policies.
c. Organization is as good as its weakest link.
d. Let employees help to determine policies and department programs.
e. Be approachable and accessible - physically and mentally.
f. Develop pleasant social relationships.

IV. WHAT IS ADMINISTRATION?

Administration is concerned with providing the environment, the material facilities, and the operational procedures that will promote the maximum growth and development of supervisors and employees. (Organization is an aspect, and a concomitant, of administration.)

There is no sharp line of demarcation between supervision and administration; these functions are intimately interrelated and, often, overlapping. They are complementary activities.

1. *PRACTICES COMMONLY CLASSED AS "SUPERVISORY"*

a. Conducting employees conferences
b. Visiting sections, units, offices, divisions, departments
c. Arranging for demonstrations
d. Examining plans
e. Suggesting professional reading
f. Interpreting bulletins
g. Recommending in-service training courses
h. Encouraging experimentation
i. Appraising employee morale
j. Providing for intervisitation

2. *PRACTICES COMMONLY CLASSIFIED AS "ADMINISTRATIVE"*

a. Management of the office
b. Arrangement of schedules for extra duties
c. Assignment of rooms or areas
d. Distribution of supplies
e. Keeping records and reports
f. Care of audio-visual materials
g. Keeping inventory records
h. Checking record cards and books
i. Programming special activities
j. Checking on the attendance and punctuality of employees

3. *PRACTICES COMMONLY CLASSIFIED AS BOTH "SUPERVISORY" AND "ADMINISTRATIVE"*
    a. Program construction
    b. Testing or evaluating outcomes
    c. Personnel accounting
    d. Ordering instructional materials

V. RESPONSIBILITIES OF THE SUPERVISOR

A person employed in a supervisory capacity must constantly be able to improve his own efficiency and ability. He represents the employer to the employees and only continuous self-examination can make him a capable supervisor.

Leadership and training are the supervisor's responsibility. An efficient working unit is one in which the employees work with the supervisor. It is his job to bring out the best in his employees. He must always be relaxed, courteous and calm in his association with his employees. Their feelings are important, and a harsh attitude does not develop the most efficient employees.

VI. COMPETENCIES OF THE SUPERVISOR

1. Complete knowledge of the duties and responsibilities of his position.
2. To be able to organize a job, plan ahead and carry through.
3. To have self-confidence and initiative.
4. To be able to handle the unexpected situation and make quick decisions.
5. To be able to properly train subordinates in the positions they are best suited for.
6. To be able to keep good human relations among his subordinates.
7. To be able to keep good human relations between his subordinates and himself and to earn their respect and trust.

VII. THE PROFESSIONAL SUPERVISOR-EMPLOYEE RELATIONSHIP

There are two kinds of efficiency: one kind is only apparent and is produced in organizations through the exercise of mere discipline; this is but a simulation of the second, or true, efficiency which springs from spontaneous cooperation. If you are a manager, no matter how great or small your responsibility, it is your job, in the final analysis, to create and develop this involuntary cooperation among the people whom you supervise. For, no matter how powerful a combination of money, machines, and materials a company may have, this is a dead and sterile thing without a team of willing, thinking and articulate people to guide it.

The following 21 points are presented as indicative of the exemplary basic relationship that should exist between supervisor and employee:

1. Each person wants to be liked and respected by his fellow employee and wants to be treated with consideration and respect by his superior.
2. The most competent employee will make an error. However, in a unit where good relations exist between the supervisor and his employees, tenseness and fear do not exist. Thus, errors are not hidden or covered up and the efficiency of a unit is not impaired.
3. Subordinates resent rules, regulations, or orders that are unreasonable or unexplained.
4. Subordinates are quick to resent unfairness, harshness, injustices and favoritism.
5. An employee will accept responsibility if he knows that he will be complimented for a job well done, and not too harshly chastised for failure; that his supervisor will check the cause of the failure, and, if it was the supervisor's fault, he will assume the blame therefore. If it was the employee's fault, his supervisor will explain the correct method or means of handling the responsibility.

6. An employee wants to receive credit for a suggestion he has made, that is used. If a suggestion cannot be used, the employee is entitled to an explanation. The supervisor should not say "no" and close the subject.
7. Fear and worry slow up a worker's ability. Poor working environment can impair his physical and mental health. A good supervisor avoids forceful methods, threats and arguments to get a job done.
8. A forceful supervisor is able to train his employees individually and as a team, and is able to motivate them in the proper channels.
9. A mature supervisor is able to properly evaluate his subordinates and to keep them happy and satisfied.
10. A sensitive supervisor will never patronize his subordinates.
11. A worthy supervisor will respect his employees' confidences.
12. Definite and clear-cut responsibilities should be assigned to each executive.
13. Responsibility should always be coupled with corresponding authority.
14. No change should be made in the scope or responsibilities of a position without a definite understanding to that effect on the part of all persons concerned.
15. No executive or employee, occupying a single position in the organization, should be subject to definite orders from more than one source.
16. Orders should never be given to subordinates over the head of a responsible executive. Rather than do this, the officer in question should be supplanted.
17. Criticisms of subordinates should, whoever possible, be made privately, and in no case should a subordinate be criticized in the presence of executives or employees of equal or lower rank.
18. No dispute or difference between executives or employees as to authority or responsibilities should be considered too trivial for prompt and careful adjudication.
19. Promotions, wage changes, and disciplinary action should always be approved by the executive immediately superior to the one directly responsible.
20. No executive or employee should ever be required, or expected, to be at the same time an assistant to, and critic of, another.
21. Any executive whose work is subject to regular inspection should, whever practicable, be given the assistance and facilities necessary to enable him to maintain an independent check of the quality of his work.

VIII. MINI-TEXT IN SUPERVISION, ADMINISTRATION, MANAGEMENT, AND ORGANIZATION

A. BRIEF HIGHLIGHTS

Listed concisely and sequentially are major headings and important data in the field for quick recall and review.

1. *LEVELS OF MANAGEMENT*

Any organization of some size has several levels of management. In terms of a ladder the levels are:

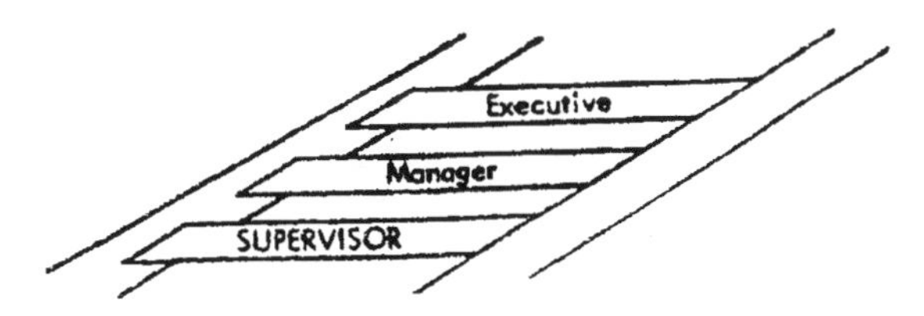

The first level is very important because it is the beginning point of management leadership.

2. *WHAT THE SUPERVISOR MUST LEARN*

A supervisor must learn to:

(1) Deal with people and their differences
(2) Get the job done through people
(3) Recognize the problems when they exist
(4) Overcome obstacles to good performance
(5) Evaluate the performance of people
(6) Check his own performance in terms of accomplishment

3. *A DEFINITION OF SUPERVISOR*

The term supervisor means any individual having authority, in the interests of the employer, to hire, transfer, suspend, lay-off, recall, promote, discharge, assign, reward, or discipline other employees or responsibility to direct them, or to adjust their grievances, or effectively to recommend such action, if, in connection with the foregoing, exercise of such authority is not of a merely routine or clerical nature but requires the use of independent judgment.

4. *ELEMENTS OF THE TEAM CONCEPT*

What is involved in teamwork? The component parts are:

(1) Members	(3) Goals	(5) Cooperation
(2) A leader	(4) Plans	(6) Spirit

5. *PRINCIPLES OF ORGANIZATION*

(1) A team member must know what his job is.
(2) Be sure that the nature and scope of a job are understood.
(3) Authority and responsibility should be carefully spelled out.
(4) A supervisor should be permitted to make the maximum number of decisions affecting his employees.
(5) Employees should report to only one supervisor.
(6) A supervisor should direct only as many employees as he can handle effectively.
(7) An organization plan should be flexible.
(8) Inspection and performance of work should be separate.
(9) Organizational problems should receive immediate attention.
(10) Assign work in line with ability and experience.

6. *THE FOUR IMPORTANT PARTS OF EVERY JOB*

(1) Inherent in every job is the *accountability* for results.
(2) A second set of factors in every job is *responsibilities.*
(3) Along with duties and responsibilities one must have the *authority* to act within certain limits without obtaining permission to proceed.
(4) No job exists in a vacuum. The supervisor is surrounded by key *relationships.*

7. *PRINCIPLES OF DELEGATION*

Where work is delegated for the first time, the supervisor should think in terms of these questions:

(1) Who is best qualified to do this?
(2) Can an employee improve his abilities by doing this?
(3) How long should an employee spend on this?
(4) Are there any special problems for which he will need guidance?
(5) How broad a delegation can I make?

8. PRINCIPLES OF EFFECTIVE COMMUNICATIONS

(1) Determine the media
(2) To whom directed?
(3) Identification and source authority
(4) Is communication understood?

9. *PRINCIPLES OF WORK IMPROVEMENT*

(1) Most people usually do only the work which is assigned to them
(2) Workers are likely to fit assigned work into the time available to perform it
(3) A good workload usually stimulates output
(4) People usually do their best work when they know that results will be reviewed or inspected
(5) Employees usually feel that someone else is responsible for conditions of work, workplace layout, job methods, type of tools/equipment, and other such factors
(6) Employees are usually defensive about their job security
(7) Employees have natural resistance to change
(8) Employees can support or destroy a supervisor
(9) A supervisor usually earns the respect of his people through his personal example of diligence and efficiency

10. *AREAS OF JOB IMPROVEMENT*

The areas of job improvement are quite numerous, but the most common ones which a supervisor can identify and utilize are:

(1) Departmental layout
(2) Flow of work
(3) Workplace layout
(4) Utilization of manpower
(5) Work methods
(6) Materials handling
(7) Utilization
(8) Motion economy

11. *SEVEN KEY POINTS IN MAKING IMPROVEMENTS*

(1) Select the job to be improved
(2) Study how it is being done now
(3) Question the present method
(4) Determine actions to be taken
(5) Chart proposed method
(6) Get approval and apply
(7) Solicit worker participation

12. *CORRECTIVE TECHNIQUES OF JOB IMPROVEMENT*

Specific Problems	General Improvement	Corrective Techniques
(1) Size of workload	(1) Departmental layout	(1) Study with scale model
(2) Inability to meet schedules	(2) Flow of work	(2) Flow chart study
(3) Strain and fatigue	(3) Work plan layout	(3) Motion analysis
(4) Improper use of men and skills	(4) Utilization of manpower	(4) Comparison of units produced to standard allowance
(5) Waste, poor quality, unsafe conditions	(5) Work methods	(5) Methods analysis
(6) Bottleneck conditions that hinder output	(6) Materials handling	(6) Flow chart & equipment study
(7) Poor utilization of equipment and machine	(7) Utilization of equipment	(7) Down time vs. running time
(8) Efficiency and productivity of labor	(8) Motion economy	(8) Motion analysis

13. A *PLANNING CHECKLIST*

(1) Objectives
(2) Controls
(3) Delegations
(4) Communications
(5) Resources
(6) Resources
(7) Manpower
(8) Equipment
(9) Supplies and materials
(10) Utilization of time
(11) Safety
(12) Money
(13) Work
(14) Timing of improvements

14. *FIVE CHARACTERISTICS OF GOOD DIRECTIONS*

In order to get results, directions must be:

(1) Possible of accomplishment
(2) Agreeable with worker interests
(3) Related to mission
(4) Planned and complete
(5) Unmistakably clear

15. *TYPES OF DIRECTIONS*

(1) Demands or direct orders
(2) Requests
(3) Suggestion or implication
(4) Volunteering

16. *CONTROLS*

A typical listing of the overall areas in which the supervisor should establish controls might be:

(1) Manpower
(2) Materials
(3) Quality of work
(4) Quantity of work
(5) Time
(6) Space
(7) Money
(8) Methods

17. *ORIENTING THE NEW EMPLOYEE*

(1) Prepare for him
(2) Welcome the new employee
(3) Orientation for the job
(4) Follow-up

18. *CHECKLIST FOR ORIENTING NEW EMPLOYEES*

	Yes	No
(1) Do your appreciate the feelings of new employees when they first report for work?	___	___
(2) Are you aware of the fact that the new employee must make a big adjustment to his job?	___	___
(3) Have you given him good reasons for liking the job and the organization?	___	___
(4) Have you prepared for his first day on the job?		
(5) Did you welcome him cordially and make him feel needed?		
(6) Did you establish rapport with him so that he feels free to talk and discuss matters with you?	___	___
(7) Did you explain his job to him and his relationship to you?	___	___
(8) Does he know that his work will be evaluated periodically on a basis that is fair and objective?	___	___
(9) Did you introduce him to his fellow workers in such a way that they are likely to accept him?	___	___
(10) Does he know what employee benefits he will receive?		
(11) Does he understand the importance of being on the job and what to do if he must leave his duty station?	___	___
(12) Has he been impressed with the importance of accident prevention and safe practice?	___	___
(13) Does he generally know his way around the department?	___	___
(14) Is he under the guidance of a sponsor who will teach the right ways of doing things?	___	___
(15) Do you plan to follow-up so that he will continue to adjust successfully to his job?	___	___

19. *PRINCIPLES OF LEARNING*
    (1) Motivation (2) Demonstration or explanation (3) Practice

20. *CAUSES OF POOR PERFORMANCE*
    (1) Improper training for job
    (2) Wrong tools
    (3) Inadequate directions
    (4) Lack of supervisory follow-up
    (5) Poor communications
    (6) Lack of standards of performance
    (7) Wrong work habits
    (8) Low morale
    (9) Other

21. *FOUR MAJOR STEPS IN ON-THE-JOB INSTRUCTION*
    (1) Prepare the worker
    (2) Present the operation
    (3) Tryout performance
    (4) Follow-up

22. *EMPLOYEES WANT FIVE THINGS*
    (1) Security (2) Opportunity (3) Recognition (4) Inclusion (5) Expression

23. *SOME DON'TS IN REGARD TO PRAISE*
    (1) Don't praise a person for something he hasn't done
    (2) Don't praise a person unless you can be sincere
    (3) Don't be sparing in praise just because your superior withholds it from you
    (4) Don't let too much time elapse between good performance and recognition of it

24. *HOW TO GAIN YOUR WORKERS' CONFIDENCE*
    Methods of developing confidence include such things as:
    (1) Knowing the interests, habits, hobbies of employees
    (2) Admitting your own inadequacies
    (3) Sharing and telling of confidence in others
    (4) Supporting people when they are in trouble
    (5) Delegating matters that can be well handled
    (6) Being frank and straightforward about problems and working conditions
    (7) Encouraging others to bring their problems to you
    (8) Taking action on problems which impede worker progress

25. *SOURCES OF EMPLOYEE PROBLEMS*
    On-the-job causes might be such things as:
    (1) A feeling that favoritism is exercised in assignments
    (2) Assignment of overtime
    (3) An undue amount of supervision
    (4) Changing methods or systems
    (5) Stealing of ideas or trade secrets
    (6) Lack of interest in job
    (7) Threat of reduction in force
    (8) Ignorance or lack of communications
    (9) Poor equipment
    (10) Lack of knowing how supervisor feels toward employee
    (11) Shift assignments

    Off-the-job problems might have to do with:
    (1) Health (2) Finances (3) Housing (4) Family

26. *THE SUPERVISOR'S KEY TO DISCIPLINE*

There are several key points about discipline which the supervisor should keep in mind:

(1) Job discipline is one of the disciplines of life and is directed by the supervisor.
(2) It is more important to correct an employee fault than to fix blame for it.
(3) Employee performance is affected by problems both on the job and off.
(4) Sudden or abrupt changes in behavior can be indications of important employee problems.
(5) Problems should be dealt with as soon as possible after they are identified.
(6) The attitude of the supervisor may have more to do with solving problems than the techniques of problem solving.
(7) Correction of employee behavior should be resorted to only after the supervisor is sure that training or counseling will not be helpful.
(8) Be sure to document your disciplinary actions.
(9) Make sure that you are disciplining on the basis of facts rather than personal feelings.
(10) Take each disciplinary step in order, being careful not to make snap judgments, or decisions based on impatience.

27. *FIVE IMPORTANT PROCESSES OF MANAGEMENT*

(1) Planning
(2) Organizing
(3) Scheduling
(4) Controlling
(5) Motivating

28. *WHEN THE SUPERVISOR FAILS TO PLAN*

(1) Supervisor creates impression of not knowing his job
(2) May lead to excessive overtime
(3) Job runs itself -- supervisor lacks control
(4) Deadlines and appointments missed
(5) Parts of the work go undone
(6) Work interrupted by emergencies
(7) Sets a bad example
(8) Uneven workload creates peaks and valleys
(9) Too much time on minor details at expense of more important tasks

29. *FOURTEEN GENERAL PRINCIPLES OF MANAGEMENT*

(1) Division of work
(2) Authority and responsibility
(3) Discipline
(4) Unity of command
(5) Unity of direction
(6) Subordination of individual interest to general interest
(7) Remuneration of personnel
(8) Centralization
(9) Scalar chain
(10) Order
(11) Equity
(12) Stability of tenure of personnel
(13) Initiative
(14) Esprit de corps

30. *CHANGE*

Bringing about change is perhaps attempted more often, and yet less well understood, than anything else the supervisor does. How do people generally react to change? (People tend to resist change that is imposed upon them by other individuals or circumstances.

Change is characteristic of every situation. It is a part of every real endeavor where the efforts of people are concerned.

A. Why do people resist change?
People may resist change because of:
(1) Fear of the unknown
(2) Implied criticism
(3) Unpleasant experiences in the past
(4) Fear of loss of status
(5) Threat to the ego
(6) Fear of loss of economic stability

B. How can we best overcome the resistance to change?
In initiating change, take these steps:
(1) Get ready to sell
(2) Identify sources of help
(3) Anticipate objections
(4) Sell benefits
(5) Listen in depth
(6) Follow up

B. BRIEF TOPICAL SUMMARIES

I. WHO/WHAT IS THE SUPERVISOR?

1. The supervisor is often called the "highest level employee and the lowest level manager."
2. A supervisor is a member of both management and the work group. He acts as a bridge between the two.
3. Most problems in supervision are in the area of human relations, or people problems.
4. Employees expect: Respect, opportunity to learn and to advance, and a sense of belonging, and so forth.
5. Supervisors are responsible for directing people and organizing work. Planning is of paramount importance.
6. A position description is a set of duties and responsibilities inherent to a given position.
7. It is important to keep the position description up-to-date and to provide each employee with his own copy.

II. THE SOCIOLOGY OF WORK

1. People are alike in many ways; however, each individual is unique.
2. The supervisor is challenged in getting to know employee differences. Acquiring skills in evaluating individuals is an asset.
3. Maintaining meaningful working relationships in the organization is of great importance.
4. The supervisor has an obligation to help individuals to develop to their fullest potential.
5. Job rotation on a planned basis helps to build versatility and to maintain interest and enthusiasm in work groups.
6. Cross training (job rotation) provides backup skills.
7. The supervisor can help reduce tension by maintaining a sense of humor, providing guidance to employees, and by making reasonable and timely decisions. Employees respond favorably to working under reasonably predictable circumstances.
8. Change is characteristic of all managerial behavior. The supervisor must adjust to changes in procedures, new methods, technological changes, and to a number of new and sometimes challenging situations.
9. To overcome the natural tendency for people to resist change, the supervisor should become more skillful in initiating change.

III. PRINCIPLES AND PRACTICES OF SUPERVISION

1. Employees should be required to answer to only one superior.
2. A supervisor can effectively direct only a limited number of employees, depending upon the complexity, variety, and proximity of the jobs involved.
3. The organizational chart presents the organization in graphic form. It reflects lines of authority and responsibility as well as interrelationships of units within the organization.
4. Distribution of work can be improved through an analysis using the "Work Distribution Chart."
5. The "Work Distribution Chart" reflects the division of work within a unit in understandable form.
6. When related tasks are given to an employee, he has a better chance of increasing his skills through training.
7. The individual who is given the responsibility for tasks must also be given the appropriate authority to insure adequate results.
8. The supervisor should delegate repetitive, routine work. Preparation of recurring reports, maintaining leave and attendance records are some examples.
9. Good discipline is essential to good task performance. Discipline is reflected in the actions of employees on the job in the absence of supervision.
10. Disciplinary action may have to be taken when the positive aspects of discipline have failed. Reprimand, warning, and suspension are examples of disciplinary action.
11. If a situation calls for a reprimand, be sure it is deserved and remember it is to be done in private.

IV. DYNAMIC LEADERSHIP

1. A style is a personal method or manner of exerting influence.
2. Authoritarian leaders often see themselves as the source of power and authority.
3. The democratic leader often perceives the group as the source of authority and power.
4. Supervisors tend to do better when using the pattern of leadership that is most natural for them.
5. Social scientists suggest that the effective supervisor use the leadership style that best fits the problem or circumstances involved.
6. All four styles -- telling, selling, consulting, joining -- have their place. Using one does not preclude using the other at another time.
7. The theory X point of view assumes that the average person dislikes work, will avoid it whenever possible, and must be coerced to achieve organizational objectives.
8. The theory Y point of view assumes that the average person considers work to be as natural as play, and, when the individual is committed, he requires little supervision or direction to accomplish desired objectives.
9. The leader's basic assumptions concerning human behavior and human nature affect his actions, decisions, and other managerial practices.
10. Dissatisfaction among employees is often present, but difficult to isolate. The supervisor should seek to weaken dissatisfaction by keeping promises, being sincere and considerate, keeping employees informed, and so forth.
11. Constructive suggestions should be encouraged during the natural progress of the work.

V. PROCESSES FOR SOLVING PROBLEMS

1. People find their daily tasks more meaningful and satisfying when they can improve them.
2. The causes of problems, or the key factors, are often hidden in the background. Ability to solve problems often involves the ability to isolate them from their backgrounds. There is some substance to the cliché that some persons "can't see the forest for the trees."
3. New procedures are often developed from old ones. Problems should be broken down into manageable parts. New ideas can be adapted from old ones.

4. People think differently in problem-solving situations. Using a logical, patterned approach is often useful. One approach found to be useful includes these steps:
   (a) Define the problem
   (b) Establish objectives
   (c) Get the facts
   (d) Weigh and decide
   (e) Take action
   (f) Evaluate action

VI. TRAINING FOR RESULTS

1. Participants respond best when they feel training is important to them.
2. The supervisor has responsibility for the training and development of those who report to him.
3. When training is delegated to others, great care must be exercised to insure the trainer has knowledge, aptitude, and interest for his work as a trainer.
4. Training (learning) of some type goes on continually. The most successful supervisor makes certain the learning contributes in a productive manner to operational goals.
5. New employees are particularly susceptible to training. Older employees facing new job situations require specific training, as well as having need for development and growth opportunities.
6. Training needs require continuous monitoring.
7. The training officer of an agency is a professional with a responsibility to assist supervisors in solving training problems.
8. Many of the self-development steps important to the supervisor's own growth are equally important to the development of peers and subordinates. Knowledge of these is important when the supervisor consults with others on development and growth opportunities.

VII. HEALTH, SAFETY, AND ACCIDENT PREVENTION

1. Management-minded supervisors take appropriate measures to assist employees in maintaining health and in assuring safe practices in the work environment.
2. Effective safety training and practices help to avoid injury and accidents.
3. Safety should be a management goal. All infractions of safety which are observed should be corrected without exception.
4. Employees' safety attitude, training and instruction, provision of safe tools and equipment, supervision, and leadership are considered highly important factors which contribute to safety and which can be influenced directly by supervisors.
5. When accidents do occur they should be investigated promptly for very important reasons, including the fact that information which is gained can be used to prevent accidents in the future.

VIII. EQUAL EMPLOYMENT OPPORTUNITY

1. The supervisor should endeavor to treat all employees fairly, without regard to religion, race, sex, or national origin.
2. Groups tend to reflect the attitude of the leader. Prejudice can be detected even in very subtle form. Supervisors must strive to create a feeling of mutual respect and confidence in every employee.
3. Complete utilization of all human resources is a national goal. Equitable consideration should be accorded women in the work force, minority-group members, the physically and mentally handicapped, and the older employee. The important question is: "Who can do the job?"
4. Training opportunities, recognition for performance, overtime assignments, promotional opportunities, and all other personnel actions are to be handled on an equitable basis.

IX. IMPROVING COMMUNICATIONS

1. Communications is achieving understanding between the sender and the receiver of a message. It also means sharing information -- the creation of understanding.
2. Communication is basic to all human activity. Words are means of conveying meanings; however, real meanings are in people.
3. There are very practical differences in the effectiveness of one-way, impersonal, and two-way communications. Words spoken face-to-face are better understood. Telephone conversations are effective, but lack the rapport of person-to-person exchanges. The whole person communicates.
4. Cooperation and communication in an organization go hand in hand. When there is a mutual respect between people, spelling out rules and procedures for communicating is unnecessary.
5. There are several barriers to effective communications. These include failure to listen with respect and understanding, lack of skill in feedback, and misinterpreting the meanings of words used by the speaker. It is also common practice to listen to what we want to hear, and tune out things we do not want to hear.
6. Communication is management's chief problem. The supervisor should accept the challenge to communicate more effectively and to improve interagency and intra-agency communications.
7. The supervisor may often plan for and conduct meetings. The planning phase is critical and may determine the success or the failure of a meeting.
8. Speaking before groups usually requires extra effort. Stage fright may never disappear completely, but it can be controlled.

X. SELF-DEVELOPMENT

1. Every employee is responsible for his own self-development.
2. Toastmaster and toastmistress clubs offer opportunities to improve skills in oral communications.
3. Planning for one's own self-development is of vital importance. Supervisors know their own strengths and limitations better than anyone else.
4. Many opportunities are open to aid the supervisor in his developmental efforts, including job assignments; training opportunities, both governmental and non-governmental -- to include universities and professional conferences and seminars.
5. Programmed instruction offers a means of studying at one's own rate.
6. Where difficulties may arise from a supervisor's being away from his work for training, he may participate in televised home study or correspondence courses to meet his self-develop- ment needs.

XI. TEACHING AND TRAINING

A. The Teaching Process

Teaching is encouraging and guiding the learning activities of students toward established goals. In most cases this process consists in five steps: preparation, presentation, summarization, evaluation, and application.

1. Preparation

Preparation is twofold in nature; that of the supervisor and the employee.
Preparation by the supervisor is absolutely essential to success. He must know what, when, where, how, and whom he will teach. Some of the factors that should be considered are:

(1) The objectives
(2) The materials needed
(3) The methods to be used
(4) Employee participation
(5) Employee interest
(6) Training aids
(7) Evaluation
(8) Summarization

Employee preparation consists in preparing the employee to receive the material. Probably the most important single factor in the preparation of the employee is arousing and maintaining his interest. He must know the objectives of the training, why he is there, how the material can be used, and its importance to him.

2. Presentation

In presentation, have a carefully designed plan and follow it.
The plan should be accurate and complete, yet flexible enough to meet situations as they arise. The method of presentation will be determined by the particular situation and objectives.

3. Summary

A summary should be made at the end of every training unit and program. In addition, there may be internal summaries depending on the nature of the material being taught. The important thing is that the trainee must always be able to understand how each part of the new material relates to the whole.

4. Application

The supervisor must arrange work so the employee will be given a chance to apply new knowledge or skills while the material is still clear in his mind and interest is high. The trainee does not really know whether he has learned the material until he has been given a chance to apply it. If the material is not applied, it loses most of its value.

5. Evaluation

The purpose of all training is to promote learning. To determine whether the training has been a success or failure, the supervisor must evaluate this learning.

In the broadest sense evaluation includes all the devices, methods, skills, and techniques used by the supervisor to keep him self and the employees informed as to their progress toward the objectives they are pursuing. The extent to which the employee has mastered the knowledge, skills, and abilities, or changed his attitudes, as determined by the program objectives, is the extent to which instruction has succeeded or failed.

Evaluation should not be confined to the end of the lesson, day, or program but should be used continuously. We shall note later the way this relates to the rest of the teaching process.

B. Teaching Methods

A teaching method is a pattern of identifiable student and instructor activity used in presenting training material.

All supervisors are faced with the problem of deciding which method should be used at a given time.

As with all methods, there are certain advantages and disadvantages to each method.

1. Lecture

The lecture is direct oral presentation of material by the supervisor. The present trend is to place less emphasis on the trainer's activity and more on that of the trainee.

2. Discussion

Teaching by discussion or conference involves using questions and other techniques to arouse interest and focus attention upon certain areas, and by doing so creating a learning situation. This can be one of the most valuable methods because it gives the employees 'an opportunity to express their ideas and pool their knowledge.

3. Demonstration

The demonstration is used to teach how something works or how to do something. It can be used to show a principle or what the results of a series of actions will be. A well-staged demonstration is particularly effective because it shows proper methods of performance in a realistic manner.

4. Performance

Performance is one of the most fundamental of all learning techniques or teaching methods. The trainee may be able to tell how a specific operation should be performed but he cannot be sure he knows how to perform the operation until he has done so.

5. Which Method to Use

Moreover, there are other methods and techniques of teaching. It is difficult to use any method without other methods entering into it. In any learning situation a combination of methods is usually more effective than anyone method alone.

Finally, evaluation must be integrated into the other aspects of the teaching-learning process.

It must be used in the motivation of the trainees; it must be used to assist in developing understanding during the training; and it must be related to employee application of the results of training.

This is distinctly the role of the supervisor.

BASIC FUNDAMENTALS OF A FINANCIAL STATEMENT

TABLE OF CONTENTS

BASIC FUNDAMENTALS OF A FINANCIAL STATEMENT

COMMENTARY

The ability to read and understand a financial statement is a basic requirement for the accountant, auditor, account clerk, bookkeeper, bank examiner, budget examiner, and, of course, for the executive who must manage and administer departmental affairs.

FINANCIAL REPORTS

Are financial reports really as difficult as all that? Well, if you know they are not so difficult because you have worked with them before, this section will be of auxiliary help for you. However, if you find financial statements a bit murky, but realize their great importance to you, we ought to get along fine together. For "mathematics," all we'll use is fourth-grade arithmetic.

Accountants, like all other professionals, have developed a specialized vocabulary. Sometimes this is helpful and sometimes plain confusing (like their practice of calling the income account, "Statement of Profit and Loss," when it is bound to be one or the other). But there are really only a score or so technical terms that you will have to get straight in mind. After that is done, the whole foggy business will begin to clear and in no time at all you'll be able to talk as wisely as the next fellow.

BALANCE SHEET

Look at the sample balance sheet printed on Page 2, and we'll have an insight into how it is put together. This particular report is neither the simplest that could be issued, nor the most complicated. It is a good average sample of the kind of report issues by an up-to-date manufacturing company.

Note particularly that the balance sheet represents the situation as it stood on one particular day, December 31, not the record of a year's operation. This balance sheet is broken into two parts on the left are shown *ASSETS* and on the right *LIABILITIES*. Under the asset column, you will find listed the value of things the company owns or are owed to the company. Under liabilities are listed the things the company owes to others, plus reserves, surplus, and the stated value of the stockholders' interest in the company.

One frequently hears the comment, "Well, I don't see what a good balance sheet is anyway, because the assets and liabilities are always the same whether the company is successful or not."

It is true that they always balance and, by itself, a balance sheet doesn't tell much until it is analyzed. Fortunately, we can make a balance sheet tell its story without too much effort–often an extremely revealing story, particularly, if we compare the records of several years.

ASSETS

The first notation on the asset side of the balance sheet is *CURRENT ASSETS* (Item 1). In general, current assets include cash and things that can be turned into cash in a hurry, or that, in the normal course of business, will be turned into cash in the reasonably near future, usually within a year.

Item 2 on our sample sheet is *CASH*. Cash is just what you would expect–bills and silver in the till and money on deposit in the bank.

UNITED STATES GOVERNMENT SECURITIES is Item 3. The general practice is to show securities listed as current assets at cost or market value, whichever is lower. The figure, for all reasonable purposes, represents the amount by which total cash could be easily increased if the company wanted to sell these securities.

The next entry is *ACCOUNTS RECEIVABLE* (Item 4). Here we find the total amount of money owed to the company by its regular business creditors and collectable within the next year. Most of the money is owed to the company by its customers for goods that the company delivered on credit. If this were a department store instead of a manufacturer, what you owed the store on our charge account would be included here. Because some people fail to pay their bills, the company sets up a reserve for doubtful accounts, which it subtracts from all the money owed.

THE ABC MANUFACTURING COMPANY, INC.
CONSOLIDATED BALANCE SHEET – DECEMBER 31

Item			Item		
1. CURRENT ASSETS			16. CURRENT LIABILITIES		
2. Cash			17. Accts. Payable		$300,000
3. U.S. Government Securities			18. Accrued Taxes		800,000
4. Accounts Receivable		2,000,000	19. Accrued Wages, interest		
(less reserves)			and Other Expenses		370,000
5. Inventories (at lower of cost or			20. Total Current Liabilities		$1,470,000
market)		2,000,000	21. FIRST MORTGAGE SINK-		
6. Total Current Assets		$7,000,000	ING FUND BONDS, 3½ %		
7. INVESTMENT IN AFFILIATED			DUE 2020		$2,000,000
COMPANY			22. RESERVE FOR		
Not consolidated (at cost, not in			CONTINGENCIES		200,000
excess of net assets)		200,000	23. CAPITAL STOCK:		
8. OTHER INVESTMENTS			24. 5% Preferred Stock		
At cost, less than market		100,000	(authorized and issued		
9. PLANT IMPROVEMENT FUND		550,000	10,000 shares of $100 par		
10. PROPERTY, PLANT AND			shares of $100		
EQUIPMENT:			(par value)	$1,000,000	
Cost	$8,000,000		25. Common stock		
11. Less Reserve			(authorized and issued		
for Depreciation	5,000,000		400,000 shares of no		
12. NET PROPERTY		3,000,000	par value)	1,000,000	
13. PREPAYMENTS		50,000	26. SURPLUS:		2,000,000
14. DEFERRED CHARGES		100,000	27. Earned	3,530,000	
15. PATENTS AND GOODWILL		100,000	28. Capital (arising from sale		
			of common capital stock		
			at price in excess of		
			stated value)	1,900,000	
					5,430,000
TOTAL		$11,000,000	TOTAL		$11,100,000

Item 5, *INVENTORIES*, is the value the company places on the supplies it owns. The inventory of a manufacturer may contain raw materials that it uses in making the things it sells, partially finished goods in process of manufacture, and, finally, completed merchandise that it is ready to sell. Several methods are used to arrive at the value placed on these various items. The most common is to value them at their cost or present market value, whichever is lower.

You can be reasonably confident, however, that the figure given is an honest and significant one for the particular industry if the report is certified by a reputable firm of public accountants.

Next on the asset side is *TOTAL CURRENT ASSETS* (Item 6). This is an extremely important figure when used in connection with other items in the report, which we will come to presently. Then we will discover how to make total current assets tell their story.

INVESTMENT IN AFFILIATED COMPANY Item 7) represents the cost to our parent company of the capital stock of its subsidiary or affiliated company. A subsidiary is simply one company that is controlled by another. Most corporations that own other companies outright lump the figures in a CONSOLIDATED BALANCE SHEET. This means that, under cash, for example, one would find a total figure that represented all of the cash of the parent company and of its wholly owned subsidiary. This is a perfectly reasonable procedure because, in the last analysis, all of the money is controlled by the same persons.

Our typical company shows that it has *OTHER INVESTMENTS* (Item 8), in addition to its affiliated company. Sometimes good marketable securities other than Government bonds are carried as current assets, but the more conservative practice is to list these other security holdings separately. If they have been bought as a permanent investment, they would always be shown by themselves. "At cost, less than market" means that our company paid $100,000 for these other investments, but they are now worth more.

Among our assets is a *PLANT IMPROVEMENT FUND* (Item 9). Of course, this item does not appear in all company balance sheets, but is typical of special funds that companies set up for one purpose or another. For example, money set aside to pay off part of the bonded debt of a company might be segregated into a special fund. The money our directors have put aside to improve the plant would often be invested in Government bonds,

FIXED ASSETS

The next item (10) is *PROPERTY, PLANT, AND EQUIPMENT*, but it might just as well be labeled Fixed Assets as these items are used more or less interchangeably, Under Item 10, the report gives the value of land, buildings, and machinery and such movable things as trucks, furniture, and hand tools. Historically, probably more sins were committed against this balance sheet item than any other.

In olden days, cattlemen used to drive their stock to market in the city. It was a common trick to stop outside of town, spread out some salt for the cattle to make them thirsty and then let them drink all the water they could hold. When they were weighed for sale, the cattlemen would collect cash for the water the stock had drunk. Business buccaneers, taking the cue from their farmer friends, would often "write up" the value of their fixed assets. In other words, they would increase the value shown on the balance sheet, making the capital stock appear to be worth a lot more than it was. *Watered stock* proved a bad investment for most stockholders. The practice has, fortunately, been stopped, though it took major financial reorganizations to squeeze the water out of some securities.

The most common practice today is to list fixed assets at cost. Often, there is no ready market for most of the things that fall under this heading, so it is not possible to give market value. A good report will tell what is included under fixed assets and how it has been valued. If the value has been increased by *write-up* or decreased by *write-down*, a footnote explanation is usually given. A *write-up* might occur, for instance, if the value of real estate increased substantially. A *write-down* might follow the invention of a new machine that put an important part of the company's equipment out of date.

DEPRECIATION

Naturally, all of the fixed property of a company will wear out in time (except, of course, non-agricultural land). In recognition of this fact, companies set up a *RESERVE FOR APPRECIATION* (Item 11). If a truck costs $4,000 and is expected to last four years, it will be depreciated at the rate of $1,000 a year.

Two other items also frequently occur in connection with depreciation–*depletion* and *obsolescence*. Companies may lump depreciation, depletion, and obsolescence under a single title, or list them separately.

Depletion is a term used primarily by mining and oil companies (or any of the so-called extractive industries). Depletion means exhaust or use up. As the oil or other natural resource is used up, a reserve is set up, to compensate for the natural wealth the company no longer owns. This reserve is set up in recognition of the fact that, as the company sells its natural product, it must get back not only the cost of extracting but also the original cost of the natural resource.

Obsolescence represents the loss in value because a piece of property has gone out of date before it wore out. Airplanes are modern examples of assets that tend to get behind the times long before the parts wear out. (Women and husbands will be familiar with the speed at which ladies' hats "obsolesce.")

In our sample balance sheet we have placed the reserve for depreciation under fixed assets and then subtracted, giving us *NET PROPERTY* (Item 12), which we add into the asset column. Sometimes, companies put the reserve for depreciation in the liability column. As you can see, the effect is just the same whether it is *subtracted* from assets or *added* to liabilities.

The manufacturer, whose balance sheet we use, rents a New York showroom and pays his rent yearly, in advance. Consequently, he has listed under assets *PREPAYMENTS* (Item 13). This is listed as an asset because he has paid for the use of the showroom, but has not yet received the benefit from its use. The use is something coming to the firm in the following year and, hence, is an asset. The dollar value of this asset will decrease by one-twelfth each month during the coming year.

DEFERRED CHARGES (Item 14) represents a type of expenditure similar to prepayment. For example, our manufacturer brought out a new product last year, spending $100,000 introducing it to the market. As the benefit from this expenditure will be returned over months or even years to come, the manufacturer did not think it reasonable to charge the full expenditure against costs during the year. He has *deferred* the charges and will write them off gradually.

INTANGIBLES

The last entry in our asset column is *PATENTS AND GOODWILL* (Item 15). If our company were a young one, set up to manufacturer some new patented product, it would probably carry its patents at a substantial figure. In fact, *intangibles* of both old and new companies are often of great but generally unmeasurable worth.

Company practice varies considerably in assigning value to intangibles. Proctor & Gamble, despite the tremendous goodwill that has been built up for *Ivory Soap*, has reduced all of its intangibles to the nominal $1. Some of the big cigarette companies, on the contrary, place a high dollar value on the goodwill their brand names enjoy. Companies that spend a good deal for research and the development of new products are more inclined than others to reflect this fact in the value assigned to patents, license agreements, etc.

LIABILITIES

The liability side of the balance sheet appears a little deceptive at first glance. Several of the entries simply don't sound like liabilities by any ordinary definition of the term.

The first term on the liability side of any balance sheet is usually *CURRENT LIABILITIES* (Item 16). This is a companion to the Current Assets item across the page and includes all debts that fall due within the next year. The relation between current assets and current liabilities is one of the most revealing things to be gotten from the balance sheet, but we will go into that quite thoroughly later on.

ACCOUNTS PAYABLE (Item 17) represents the money that the company owes to its ordinary business creditors–unpaid bills for materials, supplies, insurance, and the like. Many companies itemize the money they owe in a much more detailed fashion than we have done, but, as you will see, the totals are the most interesting thing to us.

Item 18, *ACCRUED TAXES*, is the tax bill that the company estimates it still owes for the past year. We have lumped all taxes in our balance sheet, as many companies do. However, sometimes you will find each type of tax given separately. If the detailed procedure is followed, the description of the tax is usually quite sufficient to identify the separate items.

Accounts Payable was defined as the money the company owed to its regular business creditors. The company also owes, on any given day, wages to its own employees; interest to its bondholders and to banks from which it may have borrowed money; fees to its attorneys; pensions, etc. These are all totaled under *ACCRUED WAGES, INTEREST AND OTHER EXPENSES* (Item 19).

TOTAL CURRENT LIABILITIES (Item 20) is just the sum of everything that the company owed on December 31 and which must be paid sometime in the next twelve months.

It is quite clear that all of the things discussed above are liabilities. The rest of the entries on the liability side of the balance sheet, however, do not seem at first glance to be liabilities.

Our balance sheet shows that the company, on December 31, had $2,000,000 of 3½ percent First Mortgage BONDS outstanding (Item 21). Legally, the money received by a company when it sells bonds is considered a loan to the company. Therefore, it is obvious that the company owes to the bondholders an amount equal to the face value or the *call price* of the bonds it has outstanding. The call price is a figure usually larger than the face value of the bonds at which price the company can *call* the bonds in from the bondholders and pay them off before they ordinarily fall due. The date that often occurs as part of the name of a bond is the date at which the company has promised to pay off the loan from the bondholders.

RESERVES

The next heading, *RESERVE FOR CONTINGENCIES* (Item 22) sounds more like an asset than a liability. "My reserves," you might say, "are dollars in the bank, and dollars in the bank are assets.

No one would deny that you have something there. In fact, the corporation treasurer also has his reserve for contingencies balanced by either cash or some kind of unspecified investment on the asset side of the ledger. His reason for setting up a reserve on the liability side of the balance sheet is a precaution against making his financial position seem better than it is. He decided that the company might have to pay out this money during the coming year if certain things happened. If he did not set up the "reserve," his surplus would appear larger by an amount equal to his reserve.

A very large reserve for contingencies or a sharp increase in this figure from the previous year should be examined closely by the investor. Often, in the past, companies tried to hide their true earnings by transferring funds into a contingency reserve. As a reserve looks somewhat like a true liability, stockholders were confused about the real value of their securities. When a reserve is not set up for protection against some very probable loss or expenditure, it should be considered by the investor as part of surplus.

CAPITAL STOCK

Below reserves there is a major heading, *CAPITAL STOCK* (Item 23). Companies may have one type of security outstanding, or they may have a dozen. All of the issues that represent shares of ownership are capital, regardless of what they are called on the balance sheet–preferred stock, preference stock, common stock, founders' shares, capital stock, or something else.

Our typical company has one issue of 5 percent *PREFERRED STOCK* (Item 24). It is called *preferred* because those who own it have a right to dividends and assets before the *common* stockholders–that is, the holders are in a preferred position as owners. Usually, preferred stockholders do not have a voice in company affairs unless the company fails to pay them dividends at the promised rate. Their rights to dividends are almost always *cumulative*. This simply means that all past dividends must be paid before the other stockholders can receive anything. Preferred stockholders are not creditors of the company so it cannot properly be said that the company *owes* them the value of their holdings. However, in case the company decided to go out of business, preferred stockholders would have a prior claim on anything that was left in the company treasury after all of the creditors, including the bondholders, were paid off. In practice, this right does not always mean much, but it does explain why the book value of their holdings is carried as a liability.

COMMON STOCK (Item 25) is simple enough as far as definition is concerned. It represents the rights of the ordinary owner of the company. Each company has as many owners as it has stockholders. The proportion of the company that each stockholder owns is determined by the number of shares he has. However, neither the book value of a no-par common stock, nor the par value of an issue that has a given par, can be considered as representing either the original sale price, the market value, or what would be left for the stockholders if the company were liquidated.

A profitable company will seldom be dissolved. Once things have taken such a turn that dissolution appears desirable, the stated value of the stock is generally nothing but a fiction. Even if the company is profitable as a going institution, once it ceases to function even its tangible assets drop in value because there is not usually a ready market for its inventory of raw materials and semi-finished goods, or its plant and machinery.

SURPLUS

The last major heading on the liability side of the balance sheet is *SURPLUS* (Item 26). The surplus, of course, is not a liability in the popular sense at all. It represents, on our balance sheet, the difference between the stated value of our common stock and the net assets behind the stock.

Two different kinds of surplus frequently appear on company balance sheets, and our company has both kinds. The first type listed is *EARNED* surplus (Item 27). Earned surplus is roughly similar to your own savings. To the corporation, earned surplus is that part of net income which has not been paid to stockholders as dividends. It still belongs to you, but the directors have decided that it is best for the company and the stockholders to keep it in the business. The surplus may be invested in the plant just as you might invest part of your savings in your home. It may also be in cash or securities.

In addition to the earned surplus, our company also has a *CAPITAL* surplus (Item 28) of $1,900.00, which the balance sheet explains arose from selling the stock at a higher cost per share than is given as its stated value. A little arithmetic shows that the stock is carried on the books at $2.50 a share while the capital surplus amounts to $4.75 a share. From this we know that the company actually received an average of $7.25 net a share for the stock when it was sold.

WHAT DOES THE BALANCE SHEET SHOW?

Before we undertake to analyze the balance sheet figures, a word on just what an investor can expect to learn is in order. A generation or more ago, before present accounting standards had gained wide acceptance, considerable imagination went into the preparation of balance sheets. This, naturally, made the public skeptical of financial reports. Today, there is no substantial ground for skepticism. The certified public accountant, the listing requirements of the national stock exchanges, and the regulations of the Securities and Exchange Commission have, for all practical purposes, removed the grounds for doubting the good faith of financial reports.

The investor, however, is still faced with the task of determining the significance of the figures. As we have already seen, a number of items are based, to a large degree, upon estimates, while others are, of necessity, somewhat arbitrary.

NET WORKING CAPITAL

There is one very important thing that we can find from the balance sheet and accept with the full confidence that we know what we are dealing with. That is net working capital, sometimes simply called working capital.

On the asset side of our balance sheet, we have added up all of the current assets and show the total as Item 6. On the liability side, Item 20 gives the total of current liabilities. *Net working capital* or *net current assets* is the difference left after subtracting current liabilities from current assets. If you consider yourself an investor rather than a speculator, you should always insist that any company in which you invest have a comfortable amount of working capital. The ability of a company to meet its obligations with ease, expand its volume as business expands and take advantage of opportunities as they present themselves, is, to an important degree, determined by its working capital.

Probably the question in your mind is: "*Just what does 'comfortable amount*' of working capital mean?" Well, there are several methods used by analysts to judge whether a particular company has a sound working capital position. The first rough test for an industrial company is to compare the working capital figure with the current liability total. Most analysts say that minimum safety requires that net working capital at least equal current liabilities. Or, put another way, current assets should be at least twice as large as current liabilities.

There are so many different kinds of companies, however, that this test requires a great deal of modification if it is to be really helpful in analyzing companies in different industries. To help you interpret the current position of a company in which you are considering investing, the *current ratio* is more helpful than the dollar total of working capital. The current ratio is current assets divided by current liabilities.

In addition to working capital and current ratio, there are two other ways of testing the adequacy of the current position. *Net quick assets* provide a rigorous and important test of a company's ability to meet its current obligations. Net quick assets are found by taking total current assets (Item 6) and subtracting the value of inventories (Item 5). A well-fixed industrial company should show a reasonable excess of quick assets over current liabilities.

Finally, many analysts say that a good industrial company should have at least as much working capital (current assets less current liabilities) as the total book value of its bonds and preferred stock. In other words, current liabilities, bonded debt, and preferred stock *altogether* should not exceed the current assets.

INVENTORY AND INVENTORY TURNOVER

In the recent past, there has been much talk of inventories. Many commentators have said that these carry a serious danger to company earnings if management allows them to increase too much. Of course, this has always been true, but present high prices have made everyone more inventory-conscious than usual.

There are several dangers in a large inventory position. In the first place, sharp drop in price may cause serious losses; also, a large inventory may indicate that the company has accumulated a big supply of unsalable merchandise. The question still remains, however: "What do we mean by large inventory?"

As you certainly realize, an inventory is large or small only in terms of the yearly turnover and the type of business. We can discover the annual turnover of our sample company by dividing inventories (Item 5) into total annual sales (item "a" on the income account).

It is also interesting to compare the value of the inventory of a company being studied with total current assets. Again, however, there is considerable variation between different types of companies, so that the relationship becomes significant only when compared with similar companies.

NET BOOK VALUE OF SECURITIES

There is one other very important thing that can be gotten from the balance sheet, and that is the net book or equity value of the company's securities. We can calculate the net book value of each of the three types of securities our company has outstanding by a little very simple arithmetic. *Book value* means *the value at which something is carried on the books of the company.*

The full rights of the bondholders come before any of the rights of the stockholders, so, to find the net book value or net tangible assets backing up the bonds we add together the balance sheet value of the bonds, preferred stock, common stock, reserve, and surplus. This gives us a total of $9,630,000. (We would not include contingency reserve if we were reasonably sure the contingency was going to arise, but, as general reserves are often equivalent to surplus, it is, usually, best to treat the reserve just as though it were surplus.) However, part of this value represents the goodwill and patents carried at $100,000, which is not a tangible item, so, to be conservative, we subtract this amount, leaving $9,530,000 as the total net book value of the bonds. This is equivalent to $4,765 for each $1,000 bond, a generous figure. To calculate the net book value of the preferred stock, we must eliminate the face value of the bonds, and then, following the same procedure, add the value of the preferred stock, common stock, reserve, and surplus, and subtract goodwill. This gives us a total net book value for the preferred stock of $7,530 or $753 for each share of $100 par value preferred. This is also very good coverage for the preferred stock, but we must examine current earnings before becoming too enthusiastic about the value of any security.

The net book value of the common stock, while an interesting figure, is not so important as the coverage on the senior securities. In case of liquidation, there is seldom much left for the common stockholders because of the normal loss in value of company assets when they are put up for sale, as mentioned before. The book value figure, however, does give us a basis for comparison with other companies. Comparisons of net book value over a period of years also show us if the company is a soundly growing one or, on the other hand, is losing ground. Earnings, however, are our important measure of common stock values, as we will see shortly.

The net book value of the common stock is found by adding the stated value of the common stock, reserves, and surplus and then subtracting patents and goodwill. This gives us a total net book value of $6,530,000. As there are 400,000 shares of common outstanding, each share has a net book value of $16.32. You must be careful not to be misled by book value figures, particularly of common stock. Profitable companies (Coca-Cola, for example) often show a very low net book value and very substantial earnings. Railroads, on the other hand, may show a high book value for their common stock but have such low or irregular earnings that the market price of the stock is much less than its apparent book value. Banks, insurance companies, and investment trusts are exceptions to what we have said about common stock net book value. As their assets are largely liquid (i.e., cash, accounts receivable, and marketable securities), the book value of their common stock sometimes indicates its value very accurately.

PROPORTION OF BONDS, PREFERRED AND COMMON STOCK

Before investing, you will want to know the proportion of each kind of security issued by the company you are considering. A high proportion of bonds reduces the attractiveness of both the preferred and common stock, while too large an amount of preferred detracts from the value of the common.

The *bond ratio* is found by dividing the face value of the bonds (Item 21), or $2,000,000, by the total value of the bonds, preferred stock, common stock, reserve, and surplus, or $9,630,000. This shows that bonds amount to about 20 percent of the total of bonds, capital, and surplus.

The *preferred stock ratio* is found in the same way, only we divide the stated value of the preferred stock by the total of the other five items. Since we have half as much preferred stock as we have bonds, the preferred ratio is roughly 10.

Naturally, the *common stock ratio* will be the difference between 100 percent and the totals of the bonds and preferred, or 70 percent in our sample company. You will want to remember that the most valuable method of determining the common stock ratio is in combination with reserve and surplus. The surplus, as we have noted, is additional backing for the common stock and usually represents either original funds paid in to the company in excess of the stated value of the common stock (capital surplus), or undistributed earnings (earned surplus).

Most investment analysts carefully examine industrial companies that have more than about a quarter of their capitalization represented by bonds, while common stock should total at least as much as all senior securities (bonds and preferred issues). When this is not the case, companies often find it difficult to raise new capital. Banks don't like to lend them money because of the already large debt, and it is sometimes difficult to sell common stock because of all the bond interest or preferred dividends that must be paid before anything is available for the common stockholder.

Railroads and public utility companies are exceptions to most of the rules of thumb that we use in discussing The ABC Manufacturing Company, Inc. Their situation is different because of the tremendous amounts of money they have invested in their fixed assets, their small inventories and he ease with which they can collect their receivables. Senior securities of railroads and utility companies frequently amount to more than half of their capitalization, Speculators often interest themselves in companies that have a high proportion of debt or preferred stock because of the *leverage factor*. A simple illustration will show why. Let us take, for example, a company with $10,000,000 of 4 percent bonds outstanding. If the company is earning $440,000 before bond interest, there will be only $40,000 left for the common stock ($10,000,000 at 4% equals $400,000). However, an increase of only 10 percent in earnings (to $484,000) will leave $84,000 for common stock dividends, or an increase of more than 100 percent. If there is only a small common issue, the increase in earnings per share would appear very impressive.

You have probably already noticed that a decline of 10 percent in earnings would not only wipe out everything available for the common stock, but result in the company being unable to cover its full interest on its bonds without dipping into surplus. This is the great danger of so-called high leverage stocks and also illustrates the fundamental weakness of companies that have a disproportionate amount of debt or preferred stock. Investors would do well to steer clear of them. Speculators, however, will continue to be fascinated by the market opportunities they offer.

THE INCOME ACCOUNT

The fundamental soundness of a company, as shown by its balance sheet, is important to investors, but of even greater interest is the record of its operation. Its financial structure shows much of its ability to weather storms and pick up speed when times are good. It is the income record, however, that shows us how a company is actually doing and gives us our best guide to the future.

The *Consolidated Income and Earned Surplus* account of our company is stated on the next page. Follow the items given there and we will find out just how our company earned its money, what it did with its earnings, and what it all means in terms of our three classes of securities. We have used a combined income and surplus account because it is the form most frequently followed by industrial companies. However, sometimes the two statements are given separately. Also, a variety of names are used to describe this same part of the financial report. Sometimes it is called profit and loss account, sometimes *record of earnings*, and, often, simply *income account*. They are all the same thing.

The details that you will find on different income statements also vary a great deal. Some companies show only eight or ten separate items, while others will give a page or more of closely spaced entries that break down each individual type of revenue or cost. We have tried to strike a balance between extremes; give the major items that are in most income statements, omitting details that are only interesting to the expert analyst.

The most important source of revenue always makes up the first item on the income statement. In our company, it is *Net Sales* (Item “a”). If it were a railroad or a utility instead of a manufacturer, this item would be called *gross revenues*. In any case, it represents the money paid into the company by its customers. Net sales are given to show that the figure represents the amount of money actually received after allowing for discounts and returned goods.

Net sales or gross revenues, you will note, is given before any kind of miscellaneous revenue that might have been received from investments, the sale of company property, tax refunds, or the like. A well-prepared income statement is always set up this way so that the stockholder can estimate the success of the company in fulfilling its major job of selling goods or service. If this were not so, you could not tell whether the company was really losing or making money on its operations, particularly over the last few years when tax rebates and other unusual things have often had great influence on final net income figures.

The ABC Manufacturing Company, Inc.
CONSOLIDATED INCOME AND EARNED SURPLUS
For the Year Ended December 31

Item		
a. Sales		$10,000,000
b. COST OF SALES, EXPENSES AND OTHER OPERATING CHARGES:		
c. Cost of Goods Sold	$7,000,000	
d. Selling, Administrative & Gen. Expenses	500,000	
e. Depreciation	200,000	
f. Maintenance and Repairs	400,000	
g. Taxes (Other than Federal Inc. Taxes)	300,000	
h. NET PROFIT FROM OPERATIONS		8,400,000
i. OTHER INCOME:		$1,600,000
j. Royalties and Dividends	$250,000	
k. Interest	25,000	
l. TOTAL		$1,875,000
m. INTEREST CHARGES:		
n. Interest on Funded Debt	$70,000	
o. Other Interest	20,000	90,000
p. NET INCOME BEFORE PROVISION FOR FED. INCOME TAXES		$1,785,000
q. PROVISION FOR FEDERAL INCOME TAXES		678,300
r. NET INCOME		$1,106,700
s. DIVIDENDS		
t. Preferred Stock - $5.00 Per Share	$50,000	
u. Common Stock - $1.00 Per Share	400,000	
v. PROVISION FOR CONTINGENCIES	200,000	650,000
w. BALANCE CARRIED TO EARNED SURPLUS		456,700
x, EARNED SURPLUS – JANUARY 1		3,073,000
y. EARNED SURPLUS – DECEMBER 31		$3,530,000

COST OF SALES

A general heading, *Cost of Sales, Expenses, and Other Operating Charges* (Item “b”) is characteristic of a manufacturing company, but a utility company or railroad would call all of these things *operating expenses.*

The most important subdivision is *Cost of Goods Sold* (Item “c”). Included under cost of goods sold are all of the expenses that go directly into the manufacture of the products the company sells–raw materials, wages, freight, power, and rent. We have lumped these expenses together, as many companies do. Sometimes, however, you will find each item listed separately. Analyzing a detailed income account is a pretty technical operation and had best be left to the expert.

We have shown separately, opposite "d," the *Selling, Administrative and General Expenses* of the past year. Unfortunately, there is little uniformity among companies in their treatment of these important non-manufacturing costs. Our figure includes the expenses of management; that is, executive salaries and clerical costs; commissions and salaries paid to salesmen; advertising expenses, and the like.

Depreciation ("e") shows us the amount that the company transferred from income during the year to the depreciation reserve that we ran across before as Item "11" on the balance sheet (Page 2). Depreciation must be charged against income unless the company is going to live on its own fat, something that no company can do for long and stay out of bankruptcy.

MAINTENANCE

Maintenance and Repairs (Item "f") represents the money spent to keep the plant in good operating order. For example, the truck that we mentioned under depreciation must be kept running day by day. The cost of new tires, recharging the battery, painting and mechanical repairs are all maintenance costs. Despite this day-to-day work on the truck, the company must still provide for the time when it wears out–hence, the reserve for depreciation.

You can readily understand from your own experience the close connection between maintenance and depreciation. If you do not take good care of your own car, you will have to buy a new one sooner than you would had you maintained it well. Corporations face the same problem with all of their equipment. If they do not do a good job of maintenance, much more will have to be set aside for depreciation to replace the abused tools and property.

Taxes are always with us. A profitable company always pays at least two types of taxes. One group of taxes are paid without regard to profits, and include real estate taxes, excise taxes, social security, and the like (Item "g"). As these payments are a direct part of the cost of doing business, they must be included before we can determine the *Net Profit From Operations* (Item "h").

Net Profit From Operations (sometimes called *gross profit*) tells us what the company made from manufacturing and selling its products. It is an interesting figure to investors because it indicates how efficiently and successfully the company operates in its primary purpose as a creator of wealth. As a glance at the income account will tell you, there are still several other items to be deducted before the stockholder can hope to get anything. You can also easily imagine that for many companies these other items may spell the difference between profit and loss. For these reasons, we use net profit from operations as an indicator of progress in manufacturing and merchandising efficiency, not as a judge of the investment quality of securities.

Miscellaneous Income not connected with the major purpose of the company is generally listed after net profit from operations. There are quite a number of ways that corporations increase their income, including interest and dividends on securities they own, fees for special services performed, royalties on patents they allow others to use, and tax refunds. Our income statement shows *Other Income* as Item "i," under which is shown income from *Royalties* and *Dividends* (Item "j"), and as a separate entry, *Interest* (Item "k") which the company received from its bond investments. The *Total* of other income (Item "l") shows us how much The ABC Manufacturing Company received from so-called *outside activities*. Corporations with diversified interests often receive tremendous amounts of other income.

INTEREST CHARGES

There is one other class of expenses that must be deducted from our income before we can determine the base on which taxes are paid, and that is *Interest Charges* (Item "m"). As our company has $2,000,000 worth of 3 ½ percent bonds outstanding, it will pay *Interest* on Funded Debt of $70,000 (Item "n"). During the year, the company also borrowed money from the bank, on which it, of course, paid interest, shown as *Other Interest* (Item "o").

Net Income Before Provision for Federal Income Taxes ("Item "p") is an interesting figure for historical comparison. It shows us how profitable the company was in all of its various operations. A comparison of this entry over a period of years will enable you to see how well the company had been doing as a business institution before the government stepped in for its share of net earnings. Federal taxes have varied so much in recent years that earnings before taxes are often a real help in judging business progress.

A few paragraphs back we mentioned that a profitable corporation pays two general types of taxes. We have already discussed those that are paid without reference to profits. *Provision for Federal Income Taxes* (Item "q") is ordinarily figured on the total income of the company after normal business expenses, and so appears on our income account below these charges. Bond interest, for example, as it is payment on a loan, is deducted beforehand. Preferred and common stock dividends, which are profits that go to owners of the company, come after all charges and taxes.

NET INCOME

After we have deducted all of our expenses and income taxes from total income, we get *Net Income* (Item "r"). Net income is the most interesting figure of all to the investor. Net income is the amount available to pay dividends on the preferred and common stock. From the balance sheet, we have learned a good deal about the company's stability and soundness of structure; from net profit from operations, we judge whether the company is improving in industrial efficiency. Net income tells us whether the securities of the company are likely to be a profitable investment.

The figure given for a single year is not nearly all of the store, however. As we have noted before, the historical record is usually more important than the figure for any given year. This is just as true of net income as any other item. So many things change from year to year that care must be taken not to draw hasty conclusions. During the war, Excess Profits Taxes had a tremendous effect on the earnings of many companies. In the next few years, carryback tax credits allowed some companies to show a net profit despite the fact that they had operated at a loss. Even net income can be a misleading figure unless one examines it carefully. A rough and easy way of judging how sound a figure it is would be to compare it with previous years.

The investor in stocks has a vital interest in *Dividends* (Item "s"). The first dividend that our company must pay is that on its *Preferred Stock* (Item "t"). Some companies will even pay preferred dividends out of earned surplus accumulated in the past if the net income is not large enough, but such a company is skating on thin ice unless the situation is most unusual.

The directors of our company decided to pay dividends totaling ($400,000 on the *Common Stock*, or $1 a share (Item "u"). As we have noted before, the amount of dividends paid is not determined by net income, but by a decision of the stockholders' representatives–the company's directors. Common dividends, just like preferred dividends, can be paid out of surplus if there is little or no net income. Sometimes companies do this if they have a long history of regular payments and don't want to spoil the record because of some special temporary situation that caused them to lose money. This occurs even less frequently and is more dangerous than paying preferred dividends out of surplus.

It is much more common, on the contrary, to plough earnings back into the business—a phrase you frequently see on the financial pages and in company reports. The directors of our typical company have decided to pay only $1 on the common stock, though net income would have permitted them to pay much more. They decided that the company should save the difference.

The next entry on our income account, *Provision for Contingencies* (Item "v") shows us where our reserve for contingencies arose. The treasurer of our typical company has put the provision for contingencies after dividends. However, you will discover, if you look at very many financial reports, that it is sometimes placed above net income.

All of the net income that was not paid out as dividends, or set aside for contingencies, is shown as *Balance Carried to Earned Surplus* (Item "w"). In other words, it is kept in the business. In previous years, the company had also earned more than it paid out so it had already accumulated by the beginning of the year an earned surplus of $3,073,000 (Item "x"). When we total the earned surplus accumulated during the year to that which the company had at the first of the year, we get the total earned surplus at the end of the year (Item "y"). You will notice that the total here is the same as that which we ran across on the balance sheet as Item 27.

Not all companies combine their income and surplus account. When they do not, you will find that *balance carried to surplus* will be the last item on the income account. The statement of consolidated surplus would appear as a third section of the corporation's financial report. A separate surplus account might be used if the company shifted funds for reserves to surplus during the year or made any other major changes in its method of treating the surplus account.

ANALYZING THE INCOME ACCOUNT

The income account, like the balance sheet, will tell us a lot more if we make a few detailed comparisons. The size of the totals on an income account doesn't mean much by itself. A company can have hundreds of millions of dollars in net sales and be a very bad investment. On the other hand, even a very modest profit in round figure may make a security attractive if there are only a small number of shares outstanding.

Before you select a company for investment, you will want to know something of its *margin of profit*, and how this figure has changed over the years. Finding the margin of profit is very simple. We just divide the net profit from operations (Item "h") by net sales (Item "a"). The figure we get (0.16) shows us that the company made a profit of 16 percent from operations. By itself, though, this is not very helpful. We can make it significant in two ways.

In the first place, we can compare it with the margin of profit in previous years, and, from this comparison, learn if the company excels other companies that do a similar type of business. If the margin of profit of our company is very low in comparison with other companies in the same field, it is an unhealthy sign. Naturally, if it is high, we have grounds to be optimistic.

Analysts also frequently use *operating ratio* for the same purpose. The operating ratio is the complement of the margin of profit. The margin of profit of our typical company is 16. The operating ratio is 84. You can find the operating ratio either by subtracting the margin of profit from 100 or dividing the total of operating costs ($8,400,000) by net sales ($10,000,000).

The margin of profit figure and the operating ratio, like all of those ratios we examined in connection with the balance sheet, give us general information about the company, help us judge its prospects for the future. All of these comparisons have significance for the long term as they tell us about the fundamental economic condition of the company. But you still have the right to ask: "Are the securities good investments for me now?"

Investors, as opposed to speculators, are primarily interested in two things. The first is safety for their capital and the second, regularity of income. They are also interested in the rate of return on their investment but, as you will see, the rate of return will be affected by the importance placed on safety and regularity. High income implies risk. Safety must be bought by accepting a lower return.

The safety of any security is determined primarily by the earnings of the company that are available to pay interest or dividends on the particular issues. Again, though, round dollar figures aren't of much help to us. What we want to know is the relationship between the total money available and the requirements for each of the securities issued by the company.

INTEREST COVERAGE

As the bonds of our company represent part of its debt, the first thing we want to know is how easily the company can pay the interest. From the income account we see that the company had total income of $1,875,000 (Item "1"). The interest charge on our bonds each year is $70,000 (3½ percent of $2,000,000–Item 21 on the balance sheet). Dividing total income by bond interest charges ($1,875,000 by $70,000) shows us that the company earned its bond interest 26 times over. Even after income taxes, bond interest was earned 17 times, a method of testing employed by conservative analysts. Before an industrial bond should be considered a safe investment, so our company has a wide margin of safety.

To calculate the *preferred dividend coverage* (i.e., the number of times preferred dividends were earned), we must use net income as our base, as Federal Income Taxes and all interest charges must be paid before anything is available for stockholders. As we have 10,000 shares of $100 par value of preferred stock which pays a dividend of 5 percent, the total dividend requirement for the preferred stock is $50,000 (Items 24 on the balance sheet and "t" on the income account).

EARNINGS PER COMMON SHARE

The buyer of common stocks is often more concerned with the earnings per share of his stock than he is with the dividend. It is usually earnings per share or, rather, prospective earnings per share, that influence stock market prices. Our income account does not show the earnings available for the common stock, so we must calculate it ourselves. It is net income less preferred dividends (Items "r"- "t"), or $1,056,700. From the balance sheet, we know that there are 400,000 shares outstanding, so the company earned about $2.64 per share.

All of these ratios have been calculated for a single year. It cannot be emphasized too strongly, however, that the record is more important to the investor than the report of any single year. By all the tests we have employed, both the bonds and the preferred stock of our typical company appear to be very good investments, if their market prices were not too high. The investor would want to look back, however, to determine whether the operations were reasonably typical of the company.

Bonds and preferred stocks that are very safe usually sell at pretty high prices, so the yield to the investor is small. For example, if our company has been showing about the same coverage on its preferred dividends for many years and there is good reason to believe that the future will be equally kind, the company would probably replace the old 5 percent preferred with a new issue paying a lower rate, perhaps 4 percent.

STOCK PRICES

As the common stock does not receive a guaranteed dividend, its market value is determined by a great variety of influences in addition to the present yield of the stock measured by its dividends. The stock market, by bringing together buyers and sellers from all over the world, reflects their composite judgment of the present and future value of the stock. We cannot attempt here to write a treatise on the stock market. There is one important ratio, however, that every common stock buyer considers. That is the ratio of earnings to market price.

The so-called *price-earnings ratio* is simply the earnings per share on the common stock divided into the market price. Our typical company earned $2.64 a common share in the year. If the stock were selling at $30 a share, its price-earnings ratio would be about 11.4. This is the basis figure that you would want to use in comparing the common stock of this particular company with other similar stocks.

IMPORTANT TERMS AND CONCEPTS

LIABILITIES

WHAT THE COMPANY OWES—+ RESERVES + SURPLUS + STOCKHOLDERS INTEREST IN THE COMPANY

ASSETS

WHAT THE COMPANY OWNS– + WHAT IS OWED TO THE COMPANY

FIXED ASSETS

MACHINERY, EQUIPMENT, BUILDINGS, ETC.

EXAMPLES OF FIXED ASSETS

DESKS, TABLES, FILING CABINETS, BUILDINGS, LAND, TIMBERLAND, CARS AND TRUCKS, LOCOMOTIVES AND FREIGHT CARS, SHIPYARDS, OIL LANDS, ORE DEPOSITS, FOUNDRIES

EXAMPLES OF:

PREPAID EXPENSES

PREPAID INSURANCE, PREPAID RENT, PREPAIDD ROYALTIES AND PREPAID INTEREST

DEFERRED CHARGES

AMORTIZATION OF BOND DISCOUNT, ORGANIZATION EXPENSE, MOVING EXPENSES, DEVELOPMENT EXPENSES

ACCOUNTS PAYABLE

BILLS THE COMPANY OWES TO OTHERS

BONDHOLDERS ARE CREDITORS

BOND CERTIFICATES ARE IOU'S ISSUED BY A COMPANY BACKED BY A PLEDGE

BONDHOLDERS ARE OWNERS

A STOCK CERTIFICATE IS EVIDENCE OF THE SHAREHOLDER'S OWNERSHIP

EARNED SURPLUS

INCOME PLOWED BACK INTO THE BUSINESS

NET SALES

GROSS SALES MINUS DISCOUNTS AND RETURNED GOODS

NET INCOME

= TOTAL INCOME MINUS ALL EXPENSES AND INCOME TAXES